Emmy Mott brought joy to her family and everyone who knew this little angel

Aunt Ruth.
You are loved. God Bless.
Tammy Mott

A

Journey

To

Heaven

A
Journey
To
Heaven

Tammy Brodowski Mott
Bruce Brodowski

All Scripture quotations unless otherwise marked are taken from the *Holy Bible, New American Standard Bible* Copyright © 1960, 1962, 1963, 1968, 1971, 1972, 1973, 1975, 1977, 1995 by The Lockman Foundation. Used by permission.

Scripture quotations marked "ESV" are taken from the *Holy Bible, English Standard Version.* Copyright © 2000, 2001, by Crossway Bibles, a division of Good News Publishers. Used by permission. All rights reserved.

Song Title: You Never Let Go
Writer(s): Beth Redman, Matt Redman
Song ID: 39899
Copyright © 2005 Thankyou Music (PRS) (adm. worldwide at EMICMGPublishing.com excluding Europe which is adm. By Kingswaysongs) All rights reserved. Used by permission.

ISBN: 978-0-9826581-3-0
Cover design by Lisa Hainline of Lionsgate Book Design
http://www.lionsgatebookdesign.com

Editor: Lisa Lickel Publications

Cover photo: Photographs by Julie
Credit: Photographs by Julie, 22655 Hwy 6 & 19, Cambridge Springs, Pa. 16509 (814) 398-8681
e-mail: photojulie@verizon.net
website: http://www.photojulie.com

Table of Contents

Dedication

To my little girl
Emily Mott

I will
See
You later!

Mommy

Chapter One

Waiting for Answers

February 23, 2012

Tammy

I noticed my three-year-old daughter Emmy's left eye had turned inward. She was unable to use her muscle to move her eye in any direction except inward. Her walking was different. Her balance seemed to be off and she was falling a lot. She also drooled slightly, though she'd had all of her baby teeth for years. Emmy postured her left hand as if it were arthritic. I had her squeeze my fingers. There was significant weakness on the left side compared to the right side of her body. She was like a person who'd had a stroke.

I took her to our pediatrician. They consulted with the neurological department at Children's Hospital in Pittsburgh. They agreed she needed an MRI (magnetic resonance imaging test). Due to the scheduling wait time, they suggested we take her to Pittsburgh through the emergency room. We decided it was best that my husband Dennis stay home with our other children. Mom and I made the trip with Emmy, along with an overnight bag, just in case.

We arrived at the emergency room at five o'clock p.m. I described the different signs and symptoms I had seen that day. The staff exhibited a sense of urgency, an urgency I hadn't felt until that moment. The ER was extremely busy. The frowns on their faces with their wrinkled-up foreheads were worrisome. ER intake staff scurried to the phones to make emergency calls. Then they rushed Emmy to an examining room. Doctors and nurses immediately began their examination. I hadn't processed until now that something could be seriously wrong. We waited anxiously while another emergency took priority each time Emmy was next.

The doctors decided to conduct a CT (computed tomography) scan instead while they waited for the MRI unit to become available. Emmy was so scared. I kept telling her the CT scan was just like all the pictures I take of her, but with a big camera. She just had to lay very, very still for a minute or two and then it would be over.

She loved the undersea adventure decorations of the CT room. There were fish and aquatic life everywhere, even on the big camera. Emmy was a trooper, so brave. Her eyes were wide as they expressed how terrified she felt. However, she smiled and giggled while saying, "Me okay, Mommy." I held her hand and sang her favorite lullaby, "Baby Mine" from *Dumbo*, until the CT was over. We anxiously waited for the CT scan results. I could tell by the doctor's face something was wrong. She said, "Mrs. Mott, there's a mass in Emmy's head. We need an MRI for more information."

She kept talking, but all I could hear in my mind was THERE IS A MASS IN EMMY'S HEAD. She kept mentioning a team of physicians would review the MRI results as soon as it was completed. Part of the team would be Neurological Oncology.

Wait a minute, I thought. Neurological Oncology. Do they think this mass is cancerous? How could this be? We came here to have an MRI rule out any serious issues.

I asked the question I was afraid to ask. "Are you thinking this mass is cancerous?"

"Yes, I am so sorry."

Okay, as hard as this may be, I accepted this terrible news for my daughter. It wasn't the first time I'd received this type of diagnosis before and I thought I knew what to expect.

The first year of our marriage Denny had a mass on his right hip. He went in for a biopsy. He then was asked to go into the office with me so we "could talk," which was doctor code for "we have bad news." They told us that Denny had a rare, very aggressive cancer, a peripheral nerve sheath tumor. Immediate removal was necessary. After a course of radiation, Denny remained cancer free.

But what do we do now to treat Emmy? The MRI was the next crucial step to determine exactly what we were dealing with. It was eleven-thirty p.m. and too late for an MRI. They admitted Emmy to a room for the night. The nurse asked me, "Is there anything else you need?"

What a loaded question, I thought. Did she really want to know what I needed? I needed for all of this to be over. I needed my little girl to be fine. I needed us to be home in our beds sleeping. I needed some answers to what was happening.

"Try to get some rest," she said. "They have scheduled the MRI for one p.m. tomorrow."

Emmy would not be able to eat or drink anything until it was completed. I knew she was going to be miserable waiting. I stayed up most of the night watching her sleep amongst the beeps and noises from all the attached machines. Every time I heard her little voice say, "Mommy, come sleep with me," I would move from my bed on the floor to her hospital bed.

I couldn't sleep. My mind was racing. How could this be happening? How could we lose another child? How would we get through this again? Before we adopted Emmy, our family was devastated at the loss of a foster child we'd hoped to adopt and who had returned to his birth parents.

Emmy's little life was flashing before my eyes. I thought back to her adoption day, one of the best days in my life.

Chapter Two

The Adoption of Emmy

Adoption September 2, 2009

On a summer day at the end of June 2008, the phone rang. It was Ellen from Catholic Charities calling to tell us about a baby girl who needed a temporary placement.

"Would you be interested in taking her in as a pre-adoptive foster placement child?" she asked. "The family she is staying with needs someone to take her for a weekend in July while they go away. Could you do respite care for them?"

I was so excited. It had been eighteen months since our first pre-adoptive foster child returned to his birth parents. I had prayed very hard for another child.

"I will have to talk with Denny, but I am pretty sure he will say yes," I replied.

I couldn't wait to meet what could possibly turn out to be *our* new baby girl. I contemplated how I could love someone so much since I hadn't even met her. Mom and I took the minivan to pick her up. I was anxious and nervous as we drove down the street looking for the house. We pulled up to the curb in front of the house. They opened the front door and brought out this baby girl to us.

"Oh Mom, look at her, she's so beautiful," I exclaimed.

She looked like an angel all dressed in white. She had the most beautiful sun-kissed golden color to her skin. Her dark brown hair was short and straight. Her eyes were the biggest eyes I had ever seen. With their distinctive black rims around each iris, vivid reddish orange around the pupils made them look dark brown. They slanted slightly but were so full of expression. She was plump and round. She had huge rosy red chubby cheeks. Her most distinguishing feature was her beautiful smile.

I took one look at her and couldn't help but smile back. I knew I wanted her to be mine forever.

I settled her into a car seat, smiled at my mom, and said, "I'm keeping her, she's perfect!"

We all fell in love with her. It was hard to take her back after that weekend. We counted the minutes until the day we could bring her home with us again. Days went by that turned into weeks. Weeks went by. We waited with anxious anticipation. Then, that day came on July 25, 2008. It had been twenty-nine days, twenty hours, and thirty minutes—or maybe it was thirty-two minutes—from the time she had last been with us. We were so excited, but also worried. We had been through this and in this position before. We knew about the lengthy adoption process. We knew there was a possibility her birth parents could receive custody. This whole emotional roller coaster process was something we were willing to ride again.

The legal proceedings progressed according to the court's schedule, and in November 2008 the court changed our legal goal from temporary placement to adoption. This meant the birth parents visits would discontinue and that things were moving in the right direction.

In June of 2009, a hearing occurred for termination of parental rights. The judge granted thirty days for a fact-finding hearing before he would make his decision. This process caused a lot of anxiety for us all over the past eleven months! We knew nothing was permanent until the adoption was final.

Denny and I discussed possible girl's names prior to the adoption. It took a long time to come up with a name, one on which we could both agree. We chose Emily after Denny's great-grandmother and Katherine after my great-grandmother. Her nickname would be Emmy Kate.

The waiting was excruciating. Finally, after thirteen long drawn out months, in the middle of August 2009 we received the important phone call. The judge had terminated parental rights. Now we could move forward with the adoption.

Two weeks later, September 2, 2009, was one of the best days of our lives. It took only fifteen minutes and twenty seconds—or was that thirty—for the adoption to be final. The attorney asked, "What name are you choosing for this child?" We replied, "Emily Katherine Mott." The name "Kate" never seemed to stick and she simply became our beautiful Emmy.

Chapter Three

The Diagnosis

Tammy

Nurses rushing in to get Emmy woke us in the morning. There had been a cancellation. Emmy could go at seven a.m. for the MRI.

Thank you God, we are finally moving forward towards answers.

A doctor came into the room. He looked exhausted. He had been on call for neurology all night. He seemed so young. He had brushed back his sandy blond hair. I remember he was wearing cowboy boots. They were brown leather and worn like a favorite pair of comfortable trusty reliables. I thought that wearing cowboy boots to work was unusual for a doctor. He asked me if I knew what was happening. Did I have any questions?

I asked question after question. Was this cancerous? What kind of cancer? What were our treatment options? Did she need chemo? What were the survival rates?

He said he just wasn't sure until he saw the completed MRI. He walked us down the hall towards imaging and said, "I will talk with you when you get back."

Emmy was so scared. She came out of anesthesia disoriented. She did not like the blood pressure cuff or oxygen indicator.

"Mommy, me want to go home," she repeated over and over.

"I know, baby," I said. "I want to go home too. You have been so brave. We can't go home until we talk with the doctors. We will go back to your room soon and you can watch TV and rest."

We waited for what seemed like forever. We watched a Winnie the Pooh movie and ordered sandwiches, broccoli, and fruit. Emmy ate all her food. Mom and I didn't feel like eating.

Finally, a team of physicians, nurse practitioners, and social workers came into the room. They asked me all the same questions I had answered the day before. Again, I told them our story.

The lead physician was Dr. Jakacki. "Is your husband Denny on his way?" she asked.

"No," I replied. "He is home with our boys. Does he need to be here?"

"Let's all go to a conference room and get Denny on a conference call. That way he will be available as well so that I can answer any questions he may have." Then Dr. Jakacki asked, "Why did your mother come with you instead of Denny?"

Her questioning made me feel uneasy.

"We left for Pittsburgh prior to his being able to get out of work," I said. "We felt it was best for Denny to stay at home with the boys since we weren't sure how long we would need to be in Pittsburgh.

"Our family is already under stress," I said.

Denny had undergone a follow-up medical visit at the Regional Cancer Center a couple weeks ago.

"His lymph nodes appeared abnormally enlarged. A PET scan (positron emission tomography) indicated some concern with the area around his lungs. He's scheduled for a biopsy in four days. Our twelve-year-old is autistic. We have a very active two-year-old as well. We already have so much on our plate."

"Tell me about your children," Dr. Jakacki said.

"They are all adopted," I replied. "My oldest boy is James Patrick, or JP, and is from Ukraine. We brought him home when he was twenty-two months old. The other two, Emmy and Jesse, are biological siblings. They were pre-adoptive foster-care placements through Catholic Charities Children's Services. I had three previous children placed with us as pre-adoptive placements. All of them returned to their biological families.

"As hard as it was to experience losing them, I truly feel that everything happens for a reason. If things had worked out differently with them, we wouldn't have the family we have today. We feel blessed given the opportunity to love such special children. We feel our family is finally complete."

By then Denny was on the phone for the conference call. Dr. Jakacki said, "This is what the MRI indicated. Emmy has a mass in her brain. It is a Pontine Glioma, or Brain Stem Glioma."

She handed me a book titled, *Brain Tumor Primer A Comprehensive Introduction to Brain Tumors, 9th Edition* published by the American Brain Tumor Association. This book gave extensive information regarding the symptoms and treatment options for many different types of brain tumors including DIPG (Diffuse Intrinsic Pontine Glioma), the type Emmy had.

Dr. Jakacki proceeded to discuss the facts about DIPG which were listed in the book. "[Her cancer] is located in the pons part of the brain, the area that controls connections from the brain to the spinal cord, as well as eye movements, facial muscle control, swallowing, and breathing. The tumor is diffusely infiltrating—a tumor that spreads within the area."

Dr. Jakacki's report felt like a knife was being jabbed into my heart. I felt a basketball size lump in my throat. It was hard to swallow. I could feel pools of water welling up in my eyes. I fought to hold back the tears. I couldn't breathe. I couldn't concentrate on the information she was telling me. Later, I was able to read through the book Dr. Jakacki had given me and the facts were just as horrifying.

"Surgical removal is impossible. Doing a biopsy or surgically trying to remove the tumor would essentially kill her. This type of tumor most often affects children between five and ten years old. A daily regimen of radiation treatment for six weeks, along with a steroid, could possibly take Emmy back to baseline, where she was prior to symptoms.

"The steroid would cause weight gain, a voracious appetite, and severe behavioral issues. She would need to be under anesthesia daily for the radiation treatment to occur. There is a possibility that the radiation could make things worse. If the radiation is effective, it is only temporary. The tumor will come back usually within three to six months and at that time, no course of treatment will be effective. It will be extremely aggressive.

"The average life expectancy with radiation is nine months to one year and without is only six to eight weeks."

"Her weaknesses will grow stronger. Her eyes may get worse. She will eventually no longer be able to walk. Her facial muscles will change. She will no longer be able to smile. Chewing will become more difficult. She will no longer be able to swallow. She will grow more and more tired. The little girl you now know will eventually disappear into a coma. She may develop hydrocephalus. After a week or so in a coma, she will die. As awful as this seems, the death process will be very peaceful for her."

As the lead physician, Dr. Jakacki was the only one talking. I looked around the room at the other hospital staff to see their reactions. Everyone was staring down at the table. It appeared as though they were trying to hold back their emotions. I felt like their making eye contact with me would cause them to begin crying. I was in disbelief. I couldn't fathom this was happening.

I couldn't believe what I was hearing. I had already made up my mind that we would fight this. We would get through this just as we had done before with Denny's cancer. It never occurred to me there would be no treatment. No matter what we decided to do, there was only one outcome: DEATH.

"Knowing all of this," Dr. Jakacki asked, "what step do you want to take next? There is no right or wrong decision. You need to make the decision that is best for your family and we will support you and Emmy the best that we can."

I was in a daze. I still couldn't concentrate on the doctor's remarks. I kept hoping I was in some sort of horrible nightmare and I would wake up any minute. The room seemed smaller and smaller, closing in on me. My chest hurt, my heart hurt with stabbing pains. I tried holding back the tears, wiping the corners of my eyes to keep them from running down my face, but the tears kept coming.

"Thank you for being so honest with us. We appreciate all of the facts. Tammy and I have a lot to talk about before we can give you our decision," Denny responded over the phone. I could tell from the crackle in Denny's voice that he was as upset and in as much disbelief as I.

The conference call concluded at that point. I told the team of hospital staff I was sure I knew what Denny's decision was going to be. He would not want Emmy to undergo lengthy treatments that would make her miserable when the outcome would be DEATH, but I still needed to talk to him.

I returned to Emmy's room to find her asleep. Mom was knitting.

"Well, what did they have to say?" she asked.

I replied, "It isn't good, Mom." I informed her of everything that Dr. Jakacki had told us. "Emmy's life expectancy without treatment is only six to eight weeks."

She dropped her jaw in disbelief.

"I just don't know what to do, Mom."

Her face was an expression of confusion. Her first reaction was to say we must pursue treatment. I felt she wanted us to do whatever necessary to have Emmy with us for as long as possible. She too fought back the tears. She was hurting, but wanted to be strong for Emmy and me.

As hard as it was, it was time to make some phone calls. I needed to notify family and people at work. I needed to call Dad and his wife Ellen. I needed to get all the paperwork started so I could go on family medical leave. I needed to get home so Denny and I could make one of the hardest decisions we would ever have to make in our lives. I needed to be with Denny.

I also needed some alone time. I decided to take a shower. I couldn't hold it back in anymore. The situation was so unbearable, so overwhelming. I sobbed uncontrollably, gasping for air as my limp body slumped against the shower wall. The tears kept coming and coming like waterfalls from a mountain of sorrows.

"God, haven't we been through enough already? Why is this happening to my family?" I screamed out. "You gave her to us as a precious gift. She is just a little girl. She is only three years old. My God, my God, why, why, why is this happening?"

My body shook. How could I be strong for her? Am I making the right decision? Will I question my decision later? Will I regret the choices I have made? Lord, give me the strength and wisdom to make the right decision. The decision that is best for my family.

What are we going to do now?

*****

The Phone Call

Bruce

I was in the garden when the phone rang. My wife Ellen picked up the call and came running outside with the wireless phone.

"Here," she said as she handed me the phone. "It's for you."

"Dad, it's Tammy. We're at Children's Hospital in Pittsburgh. Dad, it's not good. Emmy has Pontine Glioma, which is brain stem cancer. There's no cure, Dad. She has six to eight weeks to live."

14

I felt faint. Tears welled up in my eyes. It felt like a dagger had stabbed itself into my heart. How could God allow this to happen to my family? This was not the loving God I knew.

Ellen stood before me patiently waiting for some sign about Emmy. I put out my hand and gave her a thumb down.

"Tammy, we have a bad phone connection. Lots of static. I think I heard most of what you said. I am sorry this is happening. Are you okay?"

"I am okay, Dad. Mom is with me. I've decided that Emmy's quality of life is my top priority. Any treatments will just make her sicker and the result will still be death. I got to go, Dad. I'll talk to you later."

"Bye, Tammy, we love you."

*****

I was President of Carolinas Ecumenical Healing Ministries, which was a full-time healing prayer ministry. I have been to Brazil on a healing mission. I have seen the blind see, the lame walk, the deaf hear, and the captives set free. I believed in Matt. 8:17, which says, "This was to fulfill what was spoken through Isaiah the prophet: 'HE HIMSELF TOOK OUR INFIRMITIES AND CARRIED AWAY OUR DISEASES.'" How dared the enemy attack my family? I have VICTORY in Christ. The enemy has been defeated. This was a Declaration of War.

I handed the phone back to Ellen and stormed into the house. Throughout my life I have always found a way to do something when I have been told, "You can't."

Don't tell me I can't.

Don't tell me there was no cure.

I wanted to find a way for my granddaughter to receive medical or supernatural healing.

Google is the gateway for any researcher. More information is available on the Internet than at any other time in history.

I typed Pontine Glioma>search.

Pontine Glioma is an exceedingly rare form of terminal brainstem cancer that mostly affects the very young. Unfortunately, this cancer's statistics are beyond horrifying.

- There are only about 200 cases diagnosed each year.
- Due to the diffuse nature of the cancer there are no surgical options, and current chemotherapies have been found to be ineffective.
- With treatment, the median survival rate is less than 12 months.
- The chance of continued survival beyond 1 year is less than 8%.
- While radiation therapy does permit some relief of the symptoms, the benefits are short lived, and there are no known long-term survivors once the tumor reoccurs.

Crap, I yelled out through clenched teeth. I couldn't believe this was happening. Shaking my fist at the ceiling, I declared in my strongest voice, "Emmy's life is going to mean something. Her journey, her legacy is going to make a difference. She will not die in vain."

I spent the rest of the day putting together a Facebook page for Emmy Mott. I told people about her condition. I told people about her journey. I then requested people pray for a miracle healing for this precious little girl who had eight weeks to live. Our family never anticipated what happened next.

*****

Tammy

The doctors told us there was no possibility of a cure for this condition within the next year. I contacted St. Jude's Children's Research Hospital in Memphis, Tennessee. They'd call the next Monday to discuss options.

Dr. Jakacki decided that Emmy needed to have a Mediport inserted. The Mediport would allow access for medications. Or for treatment to make her comfortable through the progression of her disease. Her surgery was scheduled for the first thing in the morning. This procedure would be the longest of any of the other procedures or testing she had undergone. Emmy would have to undergo anesthesia again before we could return home.

"Emmy, we need to stay at the hospital one more night," I told her.

It was so hard for her to understand. "No Mommy, me want to go home. Me want Daddy, and Jesse, and JP. Me want to go home."

We tried to make it as fun as possible. We pretended that it was a girls-only sleepover. Emmy went to the hospital playroom. A dog named Elmo visited her. She loved him. "I want my own dog, Mommy. Can we take Elmo home?" she asked.

It took Emmy a little while to settle that night. She kept waking up off and on through the night. "Mommy, come sleep with me."

The next morning she was under general anesthesia longer than for the MRI. She awoke extremely disoriented. She was angry. She kept crying, "Me want to go home."

I had to restrain her to keep her from removing her blood pressure cuff and oxygen level indicator. She kept trying to remove her IV. She screamed repeatedly, "Home, Mommy, home. Me want to go home."

I wanted to take her home. It broke my heart to make her stay there. This impressed upon me how miserable and unhappy Emmy would be to have to undergo anesthesia and radiation treatment every day for six weeks.

We returned to the room. We waited for the doctors to discharge Emmy. I replayed the options in my mind Dr. Jakacki had given us the day before. I talked to one of the doctors one more time. She again reviewed the treatment options.

"I am very concerned about putting Emmy through all of the stress of treatment if it isn't going to change the outcome in the end," I said. "If we decide to have Emmy undergo treatment and it extends her life, is there a chance there will be a cure or another treatment option before she dies?"

Her answer was firm. "No, Emmy is going to die. There will be no cure during her lifetime. Deciding to undergo radiation or experimental treatments will not benefit Emmy. But it could possibly benefit another child in the future."

As much as I wanted to be able to help another child, my first priority was Emmy's quality of life. Quality of life, not Quantity.

I was sure I had made my decision

.

Chapter Four

Home

Tammy

I stopped at daycare to pick up Jesse on the way home from the hospital in Pittsburgh. Miss Vicki, the childcare staff employee, asked me if Emmy would be back at daycare.

"I'll be keeping Emmy at home," I replied. "We are going to make every moment with her as special as possible. Emmy loves Christmas and Trick or Treating."

"Can we do Trick or Treat here? Please, let us do it here at daycare," Vicki asked, full of excitement. "We can call it 'Emmy's March.' The whole school can be involved. All of the daycare children can dress up in costumes and march door to door through the school for treats. You can invite anyone you want to join us."

"Thank you so much," I said. "Emmy will be so excited."

Plans got underway. The daycare staff placed notes in all the children's mailboxes notifying their families of Emmy's March and requesting donations.

Denny and I sat down to discuss treatment options after I arrived home from daycare. We agreed that for Emmy and our family QUALITY of life was more important than quantity of life. It was an extremely hard decision, but once we finally made it, I felt a huge weight lift from my shoulders. We both agreed that we would support this decision and never look back on the "what ifs." Now we knew what we had to do to move forward. Emmy had a six to eight-week prognosis. We were determined to make those weeks the most memorable for her and our family.

On Monday, St. Jude's Children's Research Hospital called and confirmed the prognosis of Children's Hospital in Pittsburgh. They said there was nothing different that they could do that Children's Hospital couldn't. So, that was it. There were no more options.

However, we hadn't given up hope. We were all praying for a miracle. We continued to stay positive and filled our time with as many activities as possible that Emmy enjoyed. At that point she was doing well. She was happy, energetic, and loving life. Her smile lit up a room.

Denny's nieces and nephew stayed for a sleepover and we had a fire in the fireplace, camped out in the living room, made s'mores, and ate popcorn. She had a blast. She wanted to go trick or treating. We planned to do that next week with all of her friends at her daycare. Also, next week on Saturday, we would celebrate her fourth birthday, and I thought Santa might come to our house for a visit on Sunday.

So many things started happening all at once. Everyone wanted to help make Emmy's remaining time special, from Holly Hill Belgians, the family, friends, and daycare, the Make-A-Wish Foundation® to Dad, our community, and Facebook.

*****

Emmy's Facebook Page

Dad had set up a Facebook page for Emmy requesting people pray for a miracle healing. It didn't take long for news to spread about Emmy. The phone rang off the hook. People wanted to know what they could do to help. I didn't know what to tell them.

I thought about all of the things Emmy loved that she would not experience again. Christmas and Santa were two of her favorites. Word spread that we were going to have Christmas for Emmy. Presents started arriving in the mail. We put up a Christmas tree and decorated our home with Christmas lights. The neighbors thought we were all a little crazy. One of our Christmas traditions was to visit Holly Hill Belgians for a horse drawn sleigh ride. My friend Kelly Morgan contacted Sam at Holly Hill Belgians in Spartansburg. She shared our story with Sam.

"Would you be willing to do a sleigh ride for Emmy?" Kelly asked.

"Absolutely," Sam said and contacted me right away.

The next day, March 1, we went on a sleigh ride to see Santa at Cabin in the Woods. Emmy absolutely loved Santa.

*****

Going to see Santa

March 1, 2012

Emmy was so excited she was going to see Santa. She helped drive the horse-drawn sleigh to Cabin in the Woods. The ride ended at a cabin where Santa was waiting. She ran up to the cabin squealing with joy and raced to the door. Inside she heard, "Ho, Ho, Ho!"

She screamed, "Santa!" She threw open the large wooden door and ran as fast as her legs would go. Emmy jumped into Santa's arms and gave him a big kiss on the cheek. She grinned from ear to ear, quivering with excitement. I loved seeing her so happy. This was the quality of life we wanted for her. This was what we would do. We would do whatever it took to make as many special memories as possible. Memories that our family could cherish forever.

Emmy and Santa

Afterward, we all went to a restaurant for lunch. The fourteen of us had to sit at several booths and tables. Emmy wanted to sit with her Nana. The boys, Denny, and I sat at a booth. I looked around at our table. It hit me like a hard brick to my chest. This was what our family was going to look like in the future. Emmy wouldn't be sitting with us at our table.

I couldn't stop the tears from falling. I tried to hide the streams of sadness as they slowly drifted down my cheeks. I felt Denny's hand reach mine. He took one look into my eyes. He knew exactly what I was feeling and thinking. We both sat watching Emmy eat. She was at the table right beside us, but it already felt like she was so far away. I couldn't bear the thought of losing her.

Chapter Five

Emmy's March

Tammy

The day of Emmy's March finally arrived at daycare on Tuesday, March 6, 2012. Family and friends attended as well. Many of us wore costumes. I was a hotdog, Jesse a frog, and Emmy was a fierce lion. The March started in Miss Pam's classroom. She made a princess chariot with a big butterfly from a wagon for Emmy to ride in. The chariot was beautiful, but Emmy wanted to walk.

We started to march down the hallway to the room for three year-olds. Emmy was the leader. She received her treats then headed out the door to the next room. The children in each room joined in at the end of the line to participate in the march. As we headed towards the toddler rooms, I couldn't believe my eyes. The daycare had helium balloons of all colors lining the hallways. This made a path for Emmy to follow. The balloon path continued into the area for the school-age children as well. The entire school, including administrators, teachers, students, and many parents stood in the hallways to cheer us on. At each room, after they received treats, students joined in at the end of the line. Emmy could hardly carry her treat bag by the time the march ended at the gymnasium.

The gym was also decorated everywhere with colored helium balloons. There was a huge sign on the wall the kids had made that read "Emmy's March." We began with a prayer and continued with the planned program for Emmy. We all sang inspirational songs and then prayed the words from the song "You Never Let Go" by Matt Redman, from his album, *Passion: A Generation United for His Renown*, May 2008.

Even though I walk through the valley of the shadow of death,

our perfect love is casting out fear

And even when I'm caught in the middle of the storms of this life,

I won't turn back. I know you are near.

And I will fear no evil. For my God is with me and if my God is with me, whom then shall I fear? Whom then shall I fear?
And I can see a light that is coming for the heart that holds on.
A glorious light beyond all compare.
And there will be an end to these troubles.
But until that day comes, We'll live to know You here on the earth.
Yes, I can see a light that is coming for the heart that holds on.
And there will be an end to these troubles.
But until that day comes, Still I will praise You, still I will praise You.
Oh no, You never let go. Through the calm and through the storm.
Oh no, You never let go. In every high and every low.
Oh no, You never let go, Lord, You never let go of me.

I couldn't stop crying. Many people had come together. They created a moment so incredible, so spiritual, and so meaningful for a child they may not have even known. This was the beginning of a community coming together to support a child and her family. The beginning of how one child touched the hearts of so many. The beginning of an awesome journey.

Emmy at daycare for Emmy's March

Chapter Six

Let's Make a Wish

Tammy

After the doctors diagnosed Emmy and prior to us leaving Children's Hospital, a social worker met with us to discuss the Make-A-Wish® Foundation of America. He said that he would expedite a referral because of the critical time constraints. Within a week of being home, I received a call from a Make-A-Wish Foundation coordinator, Lili Morton. She made an appointment with our family to come out and meet Emmy.

Lili came to our home bearing gifts. We all received white T-shirts with navy blue letters spelling "Make a Wish." The kids received drink bottles, crayons, and markers. Emmy received a navy blue ball cap with white letters spelling "Make a Wish."

"Emmy, if you could go anywhere or do anything what would it be?" asked Lili. Emmy thought about it, but had difficulty answering. "Would you like to go see Mickey Mouse?"

Emmy's eyes lit up like a firecracker. "Yes," she exclaimed. She could hardly contain her excitement. Her body was quivering. She couldn't stop giggling or smiling. "When, when can we go?"

Lili replied, "Soon." Lili told us about the complex where Wish kids typically stay. Give Kids the World Village (GKTW) was the name. She said that it was such a treat and a special experience for families. She hoped there would be room for us to stay there since our travel time would be around Spring Break.

The last week of February, I received a call from Lili. "Tammy, we have you all set up for your trip. You will fly out of Pittsburgh International Airport March 15 and return March 21. The only disadvantage is there is no availability at GKTW. We had to set you up at another hotel. How does this work for you?"

I was disappointed that we wouldn't get to experience GKTW but I knew Emmy would have a great time wherever we stayed. I replied, "That works for us." Lili stated she put us on a cancellation list for GKTW.

Friday, March 2 I received another call from Lili. "Good news, there was a cancellation at GKTW. They have room for you to stay at the village, but we need to move your trip up a week. You will fly out of Pittsburgh March 7 and return home March 13. Will this work for you?"

I was thrilled we would get this experience. I told her we would be ready. Lili said she would come out to the house to bring our final flight itinerary and other needed information for our trip.

We needed to fly out of Pittsburgh Airport at seven-thirty a.m. on March 7. The daycare had scheduled Emmy's March for March 6. We packed ahead of time. As soon as Emmy's March was finished, we headed to Pittsburgh to stay in the Red Roof Inn. We checked in around seven-thirty p.m. We rushed to get the kids cleaned up and put to bed. We all had to be up and on the road by five a.m. in order to meet our Make-A-Wish Foundation helper at the airport. The kids were too excited. They had difficulty getting to sleep. At ten p.m., Jesse was the last to drift off to sleep. I couldn't sleep either. I was extremely anxious about flying with the children. Flying was unfamiliar territory for us. We were two parents who weren't frequent fliers, and we had a family consisting of an extremely active two-year-old, an autistic twelve-year-old, and a little three-year-old girl with brain cancer.

Denny and I hadn't flown since 2001 when we went to Ukraine to adopt JP. JP had only been on a plane to return home with us after his adoption before he was two years old. It had been a horrific trip for him. I was terrified about how JP would do on the plane due to his disability. I was worried that we didn't have enough things to occupy Emmy and Jesse for the trip. Would they sit still? Would they scream? Would they annoy other passengers? Would they be able to sit and wait during layovers when we had to transfer planes? Would we be able to handle all carry-on bags and three kids? Would we make our connecting flights? Would we be able to find GKTW once we arrived in Florida? My mind would not stop racing. It was after midnight when I finally fell asleep. Next thing I knew the alarm was going off. It was four a.m. Here we go.

I was so grateful to have a helper from Make-A-Wish Foundation at the airport. He got us through baggage check, ticket, security, and to our gate to wait for our plane. We had to wait at our gate for about an hour before we could board the plane. This was so stressful. Jesse wanted to run through the airport. JP was so nervous. He needed to keep going to the restroom. Emmy was tired, anxious, and ornery. Nothing made her happy. She was unsettled. The unknown made me stressed and the kids could feel my tension. I just wanted to get on the plane where we could strap them in and know they would be safe. Finally, they called us to board the plane. I prayed that the kids would enjoy the flight. I didn't want them to be too loud or bother other passengers.

I was pleasantly surprised. JP liked watching out the window. Emmy and Jesse were asleep before they came around to serve refreshments. The same thing happened at our two-hour layover in Washington D.C. Waiting to board our plane was so incredibly stressful. The kids were tired, cranky, and bored. It was a challenge to keep them quiet and occupied. Once we took off in the plane, the little ones fell asleep again.

I was so happy when we finally landed in Florida. I knew there would be another Make-A-Wish Foundation Volunteer to meet us and assist us in gathering our luggage and getting us a rental car. We were in our car and on our way to GKTW. We were all exhausted, but thankful to be in Florida. Denny and I kept asking each other how in the world we were ever going to make it back home without any assistance. We decided we wouldn't stress about it until we had to.

We arrived at GKTW. It looked like an amusement park from the road. Everything was so colorful. We could see a gingerbread house and a castle with a big wooden door. There was a carousel and a huge tree with a face on it that talked. It all reminded me of something from Alice in Wonderland. It looked like a magical place.

We checked into our villa. It was an actual house. We had a living room, kitchen, dining area, laundry room, two huge bedrooms, and two baths. The first thing we did after unpacking was order dinner. We could either dine at the Gingerbread House or have dinner delivered to our villa. Everyone was exhausted so we decided to order in that night.

Later, we learned the food at the Gingerbread House was out of this world. They served buffet style and had everything you could imagine. There were salad bars, hot food bars, dessert bars, and a section for kids that always had hot dogs, chicken nuggets, and macaroni and cheese.

Delivered food arrived family style. The choices were meatloaf or chicken dinners. You could also order meatloaf or chicken sandwiches, and pizza was available from eight to ten p.m. In addition to all this food there was an ice cream shack that was open pretty much all the time. We could have ice cream any way we wanted it morning, noon, and night. In addition, a cookie cart came around delivering cookies. Emmy was in her glory. Cookies and ice cream anytime she wanted, what more could she ask for?

Our first meal was meatloaf. After dinner, we got the kids settled so we could start early the next day. GKTW staff gave Denny all the information we needed for the park passes, guest passes, meal vouchers, and special activities that were happening at GKTW. Every night there was some sort of theme in which everyone could participate. Emmy was very excited about the pool at GKTW. We decided our first day we would stay at GKTW to enjoy all there was to do there.

Thursday was our first day at GKTW. We started our morning with a walk to the Gingerbread House for breakfast. We had to pass the carousel to get to the Gingerbread House. Emmy decided we needed to go to the carousel first. We were the only ones riding. Emmy didn't want to get off. We rode round and round over and over again. She loved it. I told her the carousel would be available for her to ride whenever she wanted, but we needed to be done so we could get breakfast. It took some convincing.

We finally went on to breakfast. There was a line at the Gingerbread House so we decided to eat at the Ice Cream Shack. They served continental breakfast foods for families that needed to eat quickly so they could get to the amusement parks. After breakfast, we ate ice cream. Emmy thought this was fantastic. She loved ice cream, and she was going to get as much of it as she could while we were at GKTW.

We spent our time exploring and participating in GKTW activities. One of the activities was at the Castle of Miracles. The Castle had a huge wooden door and thousands and thousands of gold stars covered the ceiling. Each star belonged to a child with a life-threatening illness who had stayed at GKTW. Emmy had a star too. We put her name on the star and put it into a slot. On a TV monitor you could see the star fairy come and take the star. At night the star fairy would take all of the stars from the day and place them on the castle ceiling. When we returned we would be able to see where the star had been placed on the ceiling.

The weather was beautiful, sunny and in the low 80s. We spent much of our day at the pool. The water was cool and refreshing. The pool had fountains that sprayed over the water and you could swim under them. Next to the pool was a water play area. You could run all through it while water shot up in the air to the rhythm of playing music. You also could run under giant mushrooms that had water streaming over them like umbrellas. There were large balancing devices that water would recycle through; fill up, and a container would tip, dumping water on anything underneath it. Emmy loved this part. She would scream, splash, run, and then come back for more. Emmy had so much fun. She didn't want to leave the village. She wanted to spend our entire week at GKTW instead of going to the amusement parks.

Friday we went to Magic Kingdom. We woke early, had breakfast at the ice cream shop and headed out on our adventure. We parked in a huge lot and rode a trolley to a tram station. We then boarded the tram and rode for two miles before we reached the entrance to Magic Kingdom. It was a very hot humid day. Being from Pennsylvania, we weren't used to the warm March weather in Florida. We rented a double stroller for Emmy and Jesse to ride. Our first stop was to see the Disney characters. Right inside the entrance was a line for children to wait to meet Daisy Duck and Pluto. Emmy couldn't wait. She was a VIP guest at the park so she moved to the front of all the lines. As soon as it was her turn she ran as fast as her little legs would take her. She gave Daisy and Pluto the biggest hugs. She had pictures taken with them both and then she got to dance with Daisy. Emmy was glowing.

Right next to Daisy and Pluto was the building where Mickey and Minnie met children. Emmy could hardly contain herself while we waited in line. She kept fidgeting and asking, "How much longer?" We were led down a narrow hallway where we waited outside a door.

There was a knock at the door. It flew open and there stood Mickey Mouse. Emmy screamed with delight. Emmy was so excited to see Mickey and Minnie. They took us inside the room where we took pictures and videos of Emmy, Jesse, and JP as they all met with Mickey and Minnie. This visit was the highlight of Emmy's day.

We spent the rest of the afternoon walking the park, watching the shows, eating lunch, buying souvenirs and riding rides. Emmy's favorite ride was "it's a small world."® She couldn't stop smiling. There was so much to see. It was hard to take it all in and not miss anything. Our day ended with a photo opportunity in front of the castle. Magic Kingdom was the perfect name for this wonderful place. It was truly magical.

We returned to GKTW for supper. We planned for "Winter Wonderland" that evening. Everything was lit up with Christmas lights. There was a snow cone maker. There were tables where kids iced sugar cookie cutouts and did Christmas arts and crafts. There were snow princesses and characters dressed as penguins, gingerbread men, and reindeer. Christmas music flowed throughout the village. Emmy loved dancing with the reindeer. Santa arrived and all the children had a turn to sit on his lap and tell him what they wanted for Christmas. After visiting with Santa, each child picked a present. The presents weren't just for Wish kids; siblings received some too. Our night ended with a horse-drawn carriage ride around the perimeter of the village. Everything was beautiful. It was a perfect ending to a perfect day.

Saturday was a very special day for our family. We had some special people come to GKTW to spend the day with us. Emmy's foster brother Gabriel and his family came to visit. Children's Services placed Gabriel as a foster child in our home one month after we received Emmy. The two of them were only five months apart in age. It was like having twins. They were inseparable and did everything together. Gabriel was a very fortunate little boy. He had a family from Florida who contacted Children's Services about Kinship care for him. When Gabriel was twenty months old, his Florida family came to Pennsylvania to take him home to live with them. It was so hard to see him go. They loved him so much. We were so thankful that Gabriel's family allowed us to remain a part of their lives. We were their Pennsylvania family, and Gabriel was and always will be Emmy's brother.

We couldn't wait to see Gabriel and get to know the rest of his family. Emmy was so excited to see him. It was the first time we had seen any of them since Gabriel left. We spent the whole day visiting, riding the carousel, eating ice cream, riding the train, eating ice cream, swimming, eating ice cream. Did I forget to mention eating ice cream? We ate a lot of ice cream. I got the cutest picture of Emmy and Gabriel from behind walking together hand in hand. It warmed my heart to see the two of them back together again.

Emmy wanted to show them the Castle of Miracles. Inside there was a playroom that looked like something from a fairyland forest. There was a well you threw tokens into and you could hear the water splash at the bottom. There was a huge mirror that displayed your face in a royal crown when you looked at the mirror's reflection.

There was so much to see and do. The best part was this was a great opportunity for all of us to find Emmy's star. GKTW staff gave us a map that showed us exactly where Emmy's star was located on the ceiling of the tower. The star fairy placed it next to thousands and thousands of other stars where its glow will remain forever as a remembrance of a very special little girl.

The entire day was perfect. We were so thankful Gabriel's family reached out to us when they heard we were coming to Florida for Emmy's Make-A-Wish Foundation trip. They made a two-hour trip to GKTW so we could all be together. Doing this meant so much to us, and I know it meant the world to Emmy. We created special memories and bonded with our Florida family. Their visit was a very, very special gift, and for that, we will be forever grateful.

Sunday was rainy. We ate breakfast and headed out to Animal Kingdom. It didn't rain, it poured. We all wore raincoats, but were still soaked from head to toe. We only spent a few hours at Animal Kingdom due to the nasty weather. We watched part of a movie from the center of a huge tree. The movie was *A Bug's Life.*

There were some interesting special effects and when it was over our seats felt like there were bugs crawling under our bottoms. We then headed to see a show called "The Lion King." It was a musical show with songs from the movie. The make-up, costumes, scenery, dancing, and singing were spectacular. I felt like I was at a show on Broadway. The rain continued to fall harder and harder. We walked to the African Safari ride. On the way, Emmy ran into the character Baloo from the *Jungle Book*. She couldn't pass up a photo opportunity with the big blue bear. The African Safari ride was outstanding. We rode in a vehicle through "Africa" where we saw elephants, giraffes, and lions. There were no barricades. It wasn't like being at the zoo. The animals were walking right among the vehicles. The giraffes were so close I could have reached out and touched one.

By lunchtime we were all soaked to the bone. We decided to head back to the GKTW village, but not before grabbing a few souvenirs on our way out.

I wasn't feeling great while we were at Animal Kingdom. By dinnertime I was sick in bed with the flu. I was so upset. I knew we only had one day left before we had to return home. We hadn't made it to Sea World. I didn't want Emmy to miss anything because of me. I prayed that whatever I had would only last twenty-four hours and by morning I would feel better.

Monday I woke feeling like a new person. I no longer felt sick to my stomach. Thank you, God! The kids and Denny ate breakfast while I got everything I could packed up for our trip home. We grabbed lunch at a drive-through on our way to Sea World. The weather was gorgeous. It was in the mid-70s. The sun was shining and the humidity was low. A gentle breeze kept us comfortable. We took out the map and planned our day according to the show times.

We had a great day. The kids loved all the animal shows. We saw Seamore and Clyde, sea lions, Shamu, and the dolphin show. We got to pet stingrays at the stingray lagoon. The kids loved this. Our favorite part of the day was feeding the dolphins at Dolphin's Cove. Emmy had the opportunity to touch and pet the dolphins while she was feeding them. She Loved this. We bought a picture of her feeding the dolphin as a remembrance of a very special day. We bought some more souvenirs then headed back to GKTW village to finish packing.

We were very anxious about our trip home. I was concerned about the amount of luggage we had. I didn't know how we were going to get all our luggage, carry-on bags, and three kids to the airport to check our luggage to make it on time for our flight home. We decided to mail half our luggage home. There was a FedEx® across the street from GKTW village. We mailed everything we wouldn't need right away. It was much cheaper than paying for extra luggage at the airport.

Tuesday morning we got up early and headed to the airport for our flight. Our feelings were bittersweet. It was hard to leave such a magical place, but we were all ready to return home. Everything went smoother than we had expected. We got all our luggage checked, cleared security, and waited at our gate to load the plane. The kids slept for both parts of our flight home. We landed in Pittsburgh, gathered our luggage, and rode on bus transport to our parked van in the parking garage. We had a two-hour drive home. It was a very long day. We were all glad to finally be home.

We were so thankful to Make-A-Wish Foundation for everything they did for our family. Our trip was magically magical, more than we could have ever hoped for. They gave us the opportunity to spend quality time enjoying each other's company in a very magical place where we didn't have to concentrate on the daily responsibilities of

36

work or home. We made very special memories that our family will be able to cherish forever. They made a little girl's dreams come true.

Mickey and Minnie Mouse with Emmy, JP, and Jesse

Chapter Seven

Emmy's Birthday Party

http://animoto.com/play/mkhAZJlkD6orVr1SCbBPXg

March 14, 2012

Tammy

Emmy was very excited about her approaching fourth birthday on April 27. I was constantly aware that Emmy had only six to eight weeks to live.

"Mommy, how much longer until I'm four?" she would ask.

The middle of April was eight weeks away. Would Emmy make it to her fourth birthday? That was all I thought about. Emmy wanted a birthday party. We decided to have an early birthday celebration.

Word spread of birthday plans for Emmy like a firestorm in the community.

The phone rang. I picked up the receiver. "Hello," I answered. The call was from my friend Laurel Andrews.

"I just heard about Emmy's birthday party. What can I do to help?" she asked.

"I don't know where to begin," I replied. "I can't come up with a date for the party."

"Well, let me know," she said before hanging up the phone.

I desired to do so much for Emmy. I was obsessed with it. The time was too short. I wanted our families to be a part of our planned activities. This meant limiting them to weekends. Only six to eight weekends gave us twelve to sixteen Saturdays and Sundays. How could I fit a lifetime of experiences into twelve to sixteen days? I paced back and forth in our large living room. I needed to think clearly. I needed a plan.

First, I needed to prioritize. Second, I needed to let others help. It was so hard for me to let others take care of details. I have always organized and have planned everything myself to the last detail. It drove my husband Denny crazy.

"Tammy, why do you have to turn everything into such a big production?" he'd ask. "Why can't things just be simple?"

Laurel kept calling me on the telephone inquiring about the birthday party. She insisted on helping and finally said, "Okay, I am planning this. Please let me do this for you. Can I please, please plan this party for Emmy?" Her voice sounded determined. She really wanted to do something to help make things a little easier for us.

There was a problem. Our home was too small to hold all the people who wanted to come celebrate. I decided to have the party at St. Anthony of Padua Church's Social Center. It had a large hall where we could set up tables at one end and all the games at the other.

Laurel contacted a group of my friends. They made all the food and drinks. The menu consisted of lasagna, meatballs for subs, meat and cheese trays for sandwiches, pasta salad, tossed garden salad and fresh bread. The beverage choices were coffee, tea, several kinds of soda, and juice boxes for the kids. They donated all of the paper products, invited seventy guests, helped with decorations, and organized games. This included a piñata, a clown, and face-painting. Meghan, my neighbor and a member of my church, volunteered to take pictures. Volunteering her time meant so much to me knowing her schedule (she was a wife, mom of three children, and a teacher) was very busy. What started out as a small family gathering turned into a huge celebration. Our friends wanted to see Emmy celebrate her birthday too.

Emmy's birthday theme was based on Nickelodeon's Dora the Explorer. The decorators covered the tables with orange tablecloths. Up the table centers were twisted lime green streamers. The centerpieces were two bundles of blue, green, and orange helium balloons attached to metallic purple weights. A "Happy Birthday" Dora banner hung as a backdrop behind the gift table. A full sheet cake brightly decorated with a Dora and Diego scene was placed at the center of a table. Festive Dora plates and napkins surrounded it. Everything was bright and colorful. Emmy's big brown eyes glowed bigger, and bigger, and bigger with excitement with each step into the hall. She squealed, "It's my birthday, it's my birthday!" as she ran around the tables. Emmy's smile lit up the room like a lighthouse beacon penetrating deep into a storm.

The amount of people who donated their time and talents to make Emmy's birthday bash a huge success amazed me. Meghan's photos were outstanding and a pleasure to look at. She posted her video on Facebook. People said they couldn't watch it without crying. Everyone wanted to help us in some way. We never anticipated how much. We will cherish this day always.

Emmy blowing out her birthday candles

Chapter Eight

Emmy's Build-A-Bear Workshop®

Tammy

We returned from Florida to one of the warmest spring days I can ever remember—in the upper 70s in the middle of March, which broke record temperatures. I took the kids to the playground at Edinboro Lake. They were all wearing shorts. We walked to the beach across the street. Both Emmy and Jesse ended up in the lake. The water was cool, but the sun was so hot. It felt refreshing. I remember saying, "This is the first time ever we've gone swimming in Northwestern Pennsylvania in March." Just two weeks before there had been snow on the ground.

My co-workers had planned a spaghetti dinner for our family. We were wearing sundresses, shorts, and tank tops. They organized a Chinese Auction. My friend's daughter, Julia, won a Visa® gift card at the auction. Her parents, Steph and John, had called to see if there was anything they could do for our family. Steph had been talking with Julia about Emmy and her prognosis. They had been praying for Emmy. Julia told Steph she thought God was making the temperatures so warm so Emmy would be able to have another summer. Such wisdom and insight for a seven-year-old. Julia decided she wanted to use the gift card she had won to take Emmy to Build-A-Bear Workshop and buy her a teddy bear. I was overcome with emotion from the love and selflessness this child was showing toward my little girl.

Emmy and I met with Julia and Steph at the mall. Emmy was very excited. She had never been to Build-A-Bear Workshop. She looked at all the choices and ended up choosing a pink flowered bunny. She picked a heart to place inside the bunny. She wanted her bunny to play music when you squeezed it. She chose "I Want Candy" from the movie *Hop*. She kept singing it over and over again. Next Emmy had the opportunity to push the button to stuff her bunny. The store employee sewed up the bunny and she was done. Off to the sink for the bunny's bath. Emmy bathed her new bunny. Then she chose outfits and accessories. It was difficult to limit her to two choices. Emmy wanted everything. She ended up choosing a summer outfit with sandals and a raincoat with matching hat and rain boots. Last, Emmy went to the computer to enter the information about her bunny. She named her bunny "Anna." After, we entered all the required information and then the computer printed out an adoption certificate. Emmy was officially Mommy to a hopping baby bunny. No bunny would be complete without hair bows and a cell phone. Of course we needed two cell phones so Jesse could have one too.

We had the best time. Julia gave Emmy a very special gift. Not only had she bought her a bunny, she gave Emmy the opportunity to experience something new, something she had never done before, something we would always remember.

Emmy and Julia at Build-A-Bear

Chapter Nine

Emmy's Christmas

March 16, 2012

Tammy

Emmy knew the schedule of events leading up to Christmas that were our family traditions. First, we went to see Santa at Cabin in the Woods. Then Santa came to our house.

"When is Santa coming, when is Santa coming?" Emmy asked daily.

The recent snow that had fallen, the trimmed tree, lights, and decorations on the house all helped to create an ambience of "Christmas" for Emmy. We picked a day when family could gather together. We told Emmy that Santa was going to come in a few days. Emmy and I counted down the days on the calendar until Emmy's "Christmas Eve." She was so excited. We made reindeer food out of oatmeal and glitter. Emmy spread the reindeer food all over the snow in our front yard.

"Me want to make sure Santa and his reindeer can find our house," she said. "Now for the cookies."

She arranged the chocolate chip cookies we made for Santa on his special plate. They were placed by the fireplace with a glass of milk. Then she ran up the stairs to her bed. Emmy was such a spitfire, so full of energy and life. I heard her little feet hit each step. I never wanted to forget that sound. One day, the sound of her little feet would be gone.

It was hard for her to fall asleep with so much excitement and anticipation for the coming of Santa. I snuggled close to Emmy, held her, and sang her lullabies. She finally drifted into sleep. She looked so beautiful. Like a peaceful angel. Would this be our last "Christmas Eve" together?

The odor of burning wood in the downstairs fireplace woke me. I loved that smell, the smell of an outdoor summer campfire, that brought back memories of camping with family and friends. I got out of bed and went downstairs. Emmy was still sleeping. I walked over and stood in front of the fireplace. The fire was so warm and inviting. I sat down and stared into the glowing light. A Thomas Kinkade Christmas DVD played on our TV. All was calm and quiet, too quiet. Quiet time for reflection made me contemplate the future. This was what my home will sound like when Emmy was gone, QUIET. Tears began to form in my eyes. I needed to get up and do something. I needed to keep busy. Staying busy, taking care of my home, taking care of my family, planning activities all kept me from thinking about the future. It was a coping mechanism for me. It was something in my life I had control of, something I could look forward to, something I could hold on to.

It was time to get breakfast ready. I put together our traditional Christmas breakfast. There was doughnuts and homemade hot cocoa with whipped cream. Our families would soon be here for breakfast and to open gifts. Denny's mom, Karen, was bringing two kinds of egg casseroles. They were a big hit at our last Christmas get together. I heard a noise upstairs.

"Denny, quick, grab the video camera. The kids are coming."

48

I took pictures of everything. I preserved every moment. Keepsakes I could treasure always. I didn't want to forget anything. Emmy came running down the stairs. Her big brown eyes were humongous with surprise when she saw all the presents Santa had put under the tree. She wiped the sleep from her eyes then looked again to be sure she wasn't dreaming.

"Santa was here, Santa was here!" she shouted with delight.

She sat and stared at her presents with amazement until everyone arrived. It took self-control for her to keep from diving into her pile of gifts. Finally, everyone arrived. We sorted the gifts into piles and passed them out. I said, "Okay everyone, let the unwrapping begin." Typically, once the green light was on, total chaos erupted. Shouting and paper flying everywhere, but not this time. Everyone intently watched Emmy open her presents. The kids were more interested in watching her reaction. What they had received wasn't important. They too were taking in every moment, imbedding each moment into their minds in order to never forget. They also realized that this might very well be Emmy's last "Christmas."

I kept thinking about the six to eight weeks she was given to live in the back of my mind. This was such a small amount of time to complete all of Emmy's favorite things—her bucket list, if you will. Emmy's "Christmas" was over. As soon as her "Christmas" dinner was finished, we took the tree down. We also put away the Christmas decorations. Out came the autumn and Halloween decorations. This was Emmy's next favorite holiday.

Dear Diary
MARCH

WEEK THREE

March 18, 2012

In the small country town of Cambridge Springs, Pennsylvania, the outpouring of love is overwhelming today. People have come from all over to donate their support at Emmy's spaghetti dinner benefit. The waiting line runs out the door into the parking area. Over 800 people are here to express their love. LOVE IS the answer. John 3:16. I will bet you that Jesus is here along with the Holy Spirit. My God, you ARE an awesome God!!!!!

WEEK FOUR

March 26, 2012

Bruce

Ellen and I travel to Tammy's house to help her organize her pictures, download her videos, and create a video of Emmy's life. There are so many pictures and videos. After two days, we are still downloading. I am finally starting to put together a video in Windows Movie Maker. It is painstaking work. Then I have to time the pictures exactly to the music. I am getting stressed out trying to get all this done this week. Tammy is getting stressed out too. Ellen and I are to leave at the end of the week for a conference in Mechanicsburg, Pennsylvania.

APRIL

WEEK FIVE

April 3 2012

Emmy is more tired the past couple days. We have been using acetaminophen and ibuprofen for headaches, which she complains of daily. Yesterday she had two episodes of dizziness. She acted as if her left side was asleep and she was about to fall over. I am hoping that this may have been due to being so tired. She had a sleepover with her Nana the night before. She stayed up a little later than usual and refused to nap. Today she seems to be doing better. She is having a little more difficulty getting around so it takes her a little longer to do things. We are going camping Thursday and Friday and she is very excited.

WEEK SIX

April 8, 2012

Emmy had to go to Pittsburgh Children's Hospital this past Thursday for a CT scan to look for any increased pressure or hydrocephalus. She has had some increased weakness on her left side and has been complaining off and on of headaches. The CT scan did not show any increased pressure or hydrocephalus. The doctors said that the scan looked similar to the one done six weeks ago, but maybe a bit more dense, which was to be expected. The doctor was surprised that Emmy was still mobile and able to walk on her own.

For now, we are going to continue to treat any headaches with acetaminophen and ibuprofen since this seems to be helping. We are going on seven weeks since the initial diagnosis and are thankful for every day we get to spend with Emmy. We will continue to try to make her smile and create as many special memories as possible. We are truly blessed. Hold your loved ones a little closer. Our time with them is so precious and sometimes shorter than we ever can imagine

April 14, 2012

Emmy's surprise birthday gift

Emmy's fourth birthday is approaching. When the doctors initially diagnosed Emmy in February, we weren't sure Emmy would make it to her actual birthday on April 27. Emmy is so excited about her birthday. She talks about it all the time. This is why we decided to throw her a birthday party in March. We wanted to be sure she had a chance to enjoy a fourth birthday while she was doing well. Now, here we are in our seventh week since diagnosis. We are all so excited to be able to celebrate Emmy's second fourth birthday.

Just before Christmas 2011, our sixteen year-old cat, Jasper, passed away. Emmy told everyone that Jasper was with baby Jesus. She asked for a pet almost every day after that.

She wants a puppy more than anything. We talk about getting the kids a puppy for Christmas. I know that with Denny and me working full time, having a special needs child, and having two children ages three and under, I would not be able to care for a puppy. It is not a good time.

We decide maybe when the kids are a little older we will have more time and they could help to care for a puppy. Emmy does not give up asking for a pet. When we tell her we can't get a puppy, she starts asking for other animals. She asks for a horse, a mouse, a guinea pig, a tiger, an elephant, a bunny, a butterfly, and the list goes on and on. Emmy loves animals. She is constantly bringing home critters she finds outside like caterpillars, spiders, worms, and slugs. She loves them all. She would talk to them and pet them. She would tell me they are her new best friends.

Emmy never gives up asking for the puppy. She tells me she wants one for her birthday. We again talk about it but I know, with everything we were dealing with, there is no way I can devote the time required to a puppy. It wouldn't be fair to the puppy. We decide we would get Emmy a kitten for her birthday. I think this will be an easy gift to find. People always have free kittens they want to give away. I search the newspapers and the Internet, but I can't find any free kittens. We stop at the Humane Society and they do not have any kittens available either. I am worried I will not be able to give Emmy a kitten for her birthday.

I decide to enlist the help of my Facebook family. I post a request for help to find a kitten for Emmy's fourth birthday. My only request is that it be a semi long-haired or long-haired kitten. I want a little fur ball Emmy can cuddle.

The response is incredible. I have message after message from people who know of available kittens. In the end we decide on a white semi long-haired kitten we adopt from Orphan Angels Cat Sanctuary. He is just six weeks old, younger than they typically let go. They want Emmy to have this kitten for her birthday. Tanya from the Riverside Health, Wellness, and Beauty Spa in Cambridge Springs helps find the kitten. She has friends on the staff at Orphan Angels and arranges for us to pick up the kitten at the Spa.

I tell Emmy we need to go to town to get her birthday surprise. We pull into the parking lot of the Riverside Spa. She is so excited. As soon as the car stops, she unbuckles her seat belt, jumps out of the minivan, and runs towards the door. Tanya greets us and leads us to the back room. Many people are waiting for us. They have decorated the room with balloons and a "Happy Birthday" banner. There is a decorated table and in the center of the table is a little brown wicker basket with a blue baby blanket. Inside the basket is the tiniest, whitest, little fur ball with big blue eyes. He jumps out of the basket and wants to play. She is so excited when she sees him. She runs in and starts petting and kissing him. She says we are taking him home and he is going to sleep with her. Then she says, "Come on, Mom, let's take him home now!" She can't wait to show her brothers and her dad. I think she is afraid she isn't going to get to keep the kitten. She wants to get him home for safekeeping. We say our thank you's and take the kitten home. Emmy needs to decide on a name for the kitten. Her favorite cartoon is *Max and Ruby* so she decides on the name Max for our new baby boy. Max is the nickname for the longer version of Maxemilyon. My mom came up with the clever spelling so it would have Emily's name in it too. MaxEMILYon.

This kitten is a true gift from God. Max and Emmy are best friends from the very first day. He cuddles in her hair and snuggles in her neck to sleep. He sleeps at her head or by her side almost every night. He is her guardian angel, her protector. He loves her very much, as she does him. He is the perfect fit for our family. As Emmy says, "He is the best birthday gift ever! Me Love, Love, Love him!"

Emmy and her new kitty Max

WEEK EIGHT

April 22, 2012

We are in week eight since her diagnosis. She is a little more tired and a bit weaker on the left side. It is more difficult for her to climb up the stairs, but it doesn't stop her. Sometimes she asks for help, but mostly wants to do it herself. It seems as though the harder things are for her, the more she insists on doing them by herself. She is a very independent child who definitely knows what she wants. She has not complained of any headaches for a couple of weeks now.

We are still getting out and about on family activities as much as she can tolerate. We are thankful for all of the beautiful weather we had last week. She spent all week outside doing her favorite things, riding her tractor, playing in the sandbox, or swimming in the hot tub.

The cold, rainy weather allows us to spend some quality family time inside too. We built a fire in the fireplace yesterday and just hung out watching her favorite shows and playing with her babies. We are so thankful for time spent together. We will continue to make Emmy smile as much as possible and cherish every day, every hour, and every minute.

April 23, 2112

Tonight, as I sit watching Emmy fall asleep, I keep thinking about precious time. We are so thankful for the extra time we have been given with Emmy, but I can't help wondering, as time goes by, how much more will she understand about what is happening to her and how hard it is going to be for all of us to eventually let go. We can't help but be excited for another day of fun activities and creating special memories, all the while realizing that every day, hour, minute, second that goes by is one step closer to the possibility of Emmy being gone from us. My heart is heavy. That said, I will stay strong, continue praying for a miracle, and continue loving time with Emmy.

MAY

WEEK TEN

May 4, 2012

It has been ten weeks since Emmy's initial diagnosis of an inoperable Pontine Glioma (brain stem tumor). We are thankful that there have not been many changes. She is still up and walking and running. She is a little more tired, but won't take naps. She is so stubborn. She was running through my mom's house the other night saying, "Look Mommy, watch how fast I can run." She has a little more weakness on the left side and isn't using her left hand for much other than support under something she is holding with her right hand. Her appetite is decreased a little, but she is still eating and chewing without any problems.

She is still the same Emmy. The biggest change is that our outings have become shorter. Because she gets tired easier, it is harder for her to go out on all-day excursions, so we try to do fun things close to home in shorter time spans. We are so thankful for every day and we will continue creating special memories and praying for a miracle.

WEEK ELEVEN

May 10, 2012

We went to Pittsburgh Children's Hospital today for an evaluation and to have Emmy's port flushed. It is so hard to take her there. She is terrified whenever we go and she cries that she just wants to go home. It breaks my heart to see her like that. The doctor couldn't believe how great she looked. She thought for sure after our last visit that Emmy would start to have increased symptoms very quickly. The doctors are amazed that she is walking and running. The doctor says that she does see some progression with the tumor, even if it is minimal, which indicates that she will eventually decline. They are unable to predict how soon it may happen, especially since she has surprised them all so far. It seems so strange talking about the changes that are supposed to happen to her as her tumor progresses. It isn't anything that we haven't heard before, but she is still doing so well that it is hard for me to believe that losing her is the prognosis.

She is a fighter and so determined. We will stay strong and keep praying for a miracle.

WEEK FOURTEEN

May 30, 2012

Today marks the end of week fourteen since Emmy's diagnosis. It is so hard to sit back and watch the changes that are happening to her and know that I can't make any of them better. As moms, that is what we are supposed to do, make everything better. I can't kiss this boo boo and make the hurt go away.

The changes that are happening are more evident now. Her balance is not great. She falls several times per day. She is frustrated that she can't get around as well as she used to. We are dealing with some difficult behaviors that I believe are related to fear. I know she is scared about what is happening to her. She doesn't understand the changes, and she doesn't have the language skills to know what questions to ask. She is pretty demanding and gets frustrated with me when I am unable to come right when she calls me.

On a positive note, her appetite is still good. She has really enjoyed being able to play outside. She loved camping over Memorial Day weekend. She was up and running around and enjoying spending time with her family. Even though she has balance problems, she is still up and walking and is generally in good spirits. She has a great sense of humor and generally says or does something every day that makes me laugh. I can't help but smile when her beautiful big brown eyes light up while she giggles and laughs at herself. She is such a character.

JUNE

WEEK SIXTEEN

June 12, 2012

Tomorrow is week sixteen. It is officially two times longer than the best prognosis given by the doctors. We are so thankful for the time we have been given. She is really enjoying all the beautiful weather and she is excited to get to swim in our pool. Unfortunately, time is starting to take its toll on her.

She is increasingly tired. She is still walking, but has much more difficulty and she falls frequently. She is still eating fine, but has started to mention that her throat feels funny and is making noises. I am wondering if swallowing is starting to feel different for her. She still has a good appetite and a great sense of humor.

She says or does something every day that seems to make me laugh. Today she told me that strawberry milkshakes are her favorite and she wants to have one every day. Her speech is harder to understand and she gets frustrated when we don't know what she is saying. The best word I can think of to describe her is unsettled. She seems to jump from one thing to the next. She has trouble finding peace or comfort in any one thing. She always wants someone with her and seems fearful if she doesn't have me in her sight at all times. I wish there was more I could do to help her to be more at peace with the changes that are happening to her. It breaks my heart to see her unhappy and afraid.

WEEK SEVENTEEN

June 20, 2012

Emmy is having a rough week. She continues to be unstable with walking due to balance issues and left side weakness. She has started to have the headaches again. Ibuprofen and acetaminophen aren't as effective as in the past. We have started to use the pain medication prescribed for her. She really does not like the taste and fights me every step of the way when taking it. It is so hard to watch her cry about her head hurting.

She ate dinner last night while sitting in my lap with her head on my shoulder and was asleep before seven p.m. She woke today feeling a little better, but has still complained on and off today of the headaches. I pray that her headaches pass quickly as they did before.

JULY

WEEK TWENTY

July 16, 2012

Emmy's headaches are much better this week. She is much more comfortable and requires less medication. Now she is having trouble with stomach pains. She has some uncomfortable stomach cramps and nausea at times. Her appetite has decreased significantly. She is taking in fluids, but has eaten very little the past four days. Today she has some yogurt, pudding, half a cheeseburger, fries and an ice cream cone. This is more than she has eaten in a week. She still complains of a tummy ache, but really has a great day. She tells me that she has a boo boo in her tummy and the doctors need to take it out so she can feel better.

We make it to the beach today, yeah! It took some convincing, but once she saw that her Aunt Ellen was coming too, she was very excited about going. It is the first smile I have seen on her little face in a while. We spend a couple hours at Presque Isle beach this afternoon. It is perfect. We couldn't have asked for a more beautiful day. The waves are big and there is a great breeze. Emmy loves the waves. She tells me she loves the beach. She has the best fun. She asks if we can stay here forever and ever. She is just too adorable.

We pick up brother Jesse from daycare and head out to get ice cream. After dinner, family and good friends stop for a visit. Emmy is so happy to have so many people come to play with her. It is a very busy day. Now my little angel is fast asleep. I think she will sleep soundly tonight.

WEEK TWENTY-TWO

July 25, 2012

Today marks the end of week twenty-two and the beginning of week twenty-three. Her headaches are less frequent and less severe. She also is not complaining of as many stomach aches. God is good.

Emmy has had some changes in mobility. She is unable to walk without holding on to furniture or total support from a person. We have a wheelchair to get her around and a hospital bed in the living room to keep her from going up and down the stairs. She is so independent and still wants to do everything herself, so she has resorted to crawling to get around on her own.

Her appetite has decreased significantly. She is beginning to lose weight. She is still taking in fluids, but her food intake is minimal. She will eat two or three bites at meals and then she is done. She has difficulty keeping food down and is getting sick every three days or so. Through all of this she remains happy and maintains her sense of humor.

Due to her muscle weakness she is unable to create her big beautiful smile. Oh, how I miss that smile, but I can tell she is happy by the way her face lights up. She is so cute when she is excited. Her giggle makes me laugh. It is harder to get her out and it usually takes some convincing, but once we go, she always has fun. Her favorite outdoor activity is still time in the pool so we are so thankful for all of our beautiful warm weather.

We will continue creating special memories and cherishing every moment. This past Monday she said, "Mom, can we go to McDonald's?" So off we went for a cheeseburger Happy Meal with chocolate milk. All night she kept telling me, "Me love, love, love McDonald's chocolate milk." It really is the little things.

Jesse pushing Emmy's wheel chair.

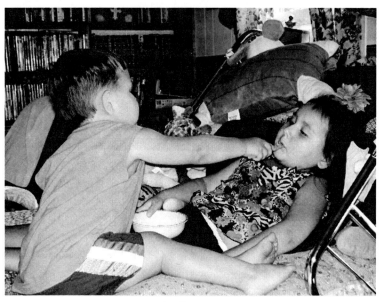

Jesse feeding Emmy

WEEK TWENTY-THREE

July 28, 2012

Emmy took a turn for the worse last night. She was very lethargic and unable to swallow. She was very restless all night and could not sleep. After administering several doses of her medication, she finally fell asleep about four a.m. but was back up at six. She is unable to talk and seems very uncomfortable and restless.

I call Hospice in to see her. After consulting with the doctors in Pittsburgh, they have changed her medications to try to make her more comfortable. Emmy finally fell asleep again around eleven-thirty a.m. and has been sleeping ever since. Her breathing is very labored. She has a lot of fluid in her throat and chest, which causes a loud rattling. She has started to run a temperature. Her oxygen levels are extremely low, reading at fifty-eight percent, and her fingertips and lips are turning blue. She is now on oxygen and her coloring is a little better. Even with the new medication to help with the fluid buildup, her breathing is still labored with a loud rattle.

What we don't know is if she is sleeping now due to the medications or if she is now in an unresponsive state. If it is God's will to call her home, we pray that this next part of her journey is as comfortable and peaceful as possible for her.

July 29, 2012

Emmy seems to be doing a little better today. She is still sleeping peacefully. Her breathing is much better and the rattle of congestion seems to be gone. Her coloring looks good and the blue in her fingertips and lips is gone. She was able to cough last night on her own, expelling some of her fluid.

I have seen a little responsiveness today. She moves her fingers and toes. I feel her squeeze my hand from time to time when I am holding it. She moves her head around when I am talking to her and she has opened her eyes a couple of times. I am hopeful that once she rests she will awaken after the medications wear off. Hopefully, we will be able to talk to her again. Her little body has been through a lot over the past forty-eight hours

July 30, 2012

Emily finally wakes at five a.m. this morning. She is restless and groggy. How wonderful to see her beautiful big brown eyes looking at me and hearing me talk to her. She can't talk, but shakes her head yes or no to several questions I ask. She wants me to crawl in bed with her. She keeps clearing her throat. The first thing she says using sign language is that she wants to eat and drink something. I am so glad we learned a little sign language when she was a baby for her to communicate now. We don't try to eat, but she drinks an entire sippy cup of ice water. She swallows without difficulty. She is up until a little after seven a.m., dozing on and off. She is breathing comfortably without oxygen. She is now sleeping peacefully.

July 31, 2012

Emmy wakes at three forty-five a.m. for a drink and goes back to sleep until nine a.m. She is alert this morning, not as groggy as she has been the past couple days. She asks for four different kinds of beverage, including her dad's coffee. She also eats half of a jar of apple banana with mixed cereal baby food. While awake, she is restless. She complains a little of tummy pain, and ends up throwing up. She is able to continue drinking throughout the day and it all stayed down.

She talks today, and I am able to understand most of what she is saying. She is weak and her spoken words are very soft. Listening to her little voice is like music to my ears. The sound is so beautiful. We are all so excited. I know she is feeling a little better when her brother Jesse comes in to see her (annoy her) this morning and she pushes him away and says, "Stop." Ah, sibling love.

She is awake for about three hours before she falls back asleep. She dozes on and off throughout the day. She became extremely drowsy again after taking her medication and has slept most of the evening. She gave us quite a scare Saturday. I am so thankful that we have had the chance to talk with her again. My family is truly blessed.

AUGUST

August 1, 2012

Emmy is having a pretty good day today. She is up for several hours this afternoon. She eats a little, it all stays down, and she drinks quite a bit. She is still groggy all day and her speech is really difficult to understand, which is so frustrating for her. I feel so bad that I can't figure out what she is saying, but we are getting pretty good at charades.

Around six-thirty p.m. she begins to exhibit signs of being uncomfortable. Her breathing seems a bit shallow and her temperature reaches 103 degrees. I give her some additional medication which brings her temp down to 101 degrees, but at eight-thirty p.m. she is still pretty anxious and uncomfortable.

I call Hospice and they give me some suggestions of what to try with her meds and by nine-fifteen she is sleeping comfortably. Her temperature is down to 99.4 degrees. I pray she will remain comfortable through the night so she can get some rest.

August 2, 2012

It is going to be a rough day today. Emmy wakes at four thirty a.m. very restless, and complaining of headaches and tummy aches. By seven-fifteen she is back asleep. She wakes back up at eleven forty-five. Her entire day has been extremely restless. She just can't seem to get comfortable. She is very fidgety, constantly moving, itching all over, reaching for something, asking for one thing and then changing her mind to another. Nothing seems to make her content. She is fighting sleep tonight. She can't seem to settle. She says she doesn't want to fall asleep. I rock her in the rocking chair for an hour and a half before she finally settles to sleep.

I put her back in her bed and she becomes restless again. She has been awake since eleven-fifteen a.m. I am guessing that once she finally falls asleep, she will sleep for awhile. It looks like it could be a long night. I am praying that she finds peace and comfort so that she can get some rest.

August 3, 2012

Emmy rested soundly from twelve forty-five to five a.m. She wakes up a little restless, but much better than yesterday. She is up watching her favorite cartoons, and is not complaining of anything bothering her. She looks exhausted, but she just won't give in to falling asleep. I hope that today will be better than yesterday.

Emmy finally falls asleep at four thirty this afternoon and is sleeping comfortably. Hospice is here for a visit today. They flush her port and do a straight catheter to get a urine sample. The lab results indicate Emmy has a urinary tract infection (UTI). Bless her little heart. It is no wonder she has been so uncomfortable and unable to sleep. She is now on antibiotics. I hope that will make her more comfortable.

She has been itching and scratching nonstop the past couple of days, so we have also given her Benadryl®. Between the Benadryl®, the rest of her medications, lack of sleep, and her recent discomfort, I am guessing that Emmy will sleep until tomorrow morning. Tonight should be a good night for all of us to get some rest. I hope that she will awake feeling a little better.

August 4, 2012

Emmy seems to be doing better today. She is not nearly as uncomfortable. She slept from yesterday around four thirty p.m. until five a.m. this morning. She fell back asleep at ten and slept until two p.m. She has been up since then so she should sleep well tonight. She is groggy and mumbles a lot when she talks, which makes it difficult to understand her. She gets so frustrated with us when we don't know what she is saying. The antibiotic must be helping. She asks to go outside this evening.

We take her for a walk around the yard in her wheelchair and then she is ready to go back in. The outing is brief, but at least she got out of bed and outside to enjoy the beautiful weather. She enjoys feeding the fish in the water garden.

When we get back inside, she wants to sit on the couch. This is the first time she has been out her of bed (except for baths) since last Friday. Now we just need to get her eating a little more so she can get some strength back. She is so tired and weak. Good thing she has a nice reserve to last her until she is ready to eat. She has lost weight, but she still has some chub to her.

August 5, 2012

Emmy sleeps on and off throughout the day today. When she is awake, she seems much more alert. Her speech is more understandable and her eyes are wide open and bright. Her coloring is better too. She does not complain of any aches or pains today. She did get sick after taking her antibiotic tonight. She really doesn't like the taste and it causes a gag reflex even after chasing it with a drink. Her eating is minimal, but she is drinking a lot of fluids.

August 8, 2012

This is our Week Twenty-four update, yeah! I really thought we were going to lose her a couple weeks ago, but she has bounced back. The antibiotic makes her feel much better. The medication she takes to make her feel more comfortable has been reduced significantly so she isn't groggy all the time.

Her sleep patterns are a bit off. She has been up more at night, and sleeping on and off through the day. Today is the first time in awhile that she woke at a normal time and is up all day. She is asleep now, so maybe she will sleep all night. She isn't eating much, but she is starting to ask for food again. Yesterday she wanted some spaghetti. She sat at the dinner table while I got supper ready and ate with the entire family. Today for lunch she eats half a hot dog and bun. This is more than she has eaten in a week. Everything stays down and there are no complaints of tummy issues.

She isn't walking at all. She moves from her bed to the couch to her chair, but she relies on us to move her from place to place. Her spirits are good and I even heard her do some giggling the past couple days. I sure have missed her silly belly laugh. Listening to it was like music to my ears. We are so thankful that God has given us more quality time with Emmy. What a blessing she is to our lives. She is our miracle.

WEEK TWENTY-FIVE

August 15, 2012

Emmy initially had a six-eight week prognosis and here we are, six months later. Thank you, Lord, for such precious time.

She is eating more and taking in fluids. Her favorite meal now is oatmeal. She eats a different flavor for breakfast, lunch and dinner. She still likes to sneak in a little ice cream now and then.

She isn't walking at all and hasn't wanted to stray too far from home. She tires easily and feels most comfortable resting in her bed. She is a bit more tired than usual, but we had a big day.

We went out to Cold Stone Creamery for yummy milk shakes. We also meet the participants for the Ride4thEm benefit that took place at the end of July. We are honored that they choose Emily as one of the children they want to sponsor. They give freely of their time and talents raising money to help families who have a child with a life threatening illness. We unfortunately were not able to attend the benefit since Emmy was having a rough time then. There really are angels among us.

SEPTEMBER

WEEK TWENTY-EIGHT

September 5, 2012

Today ends week twenty-eight. Emmy seems to be in her honeymoon stage of her disease where she seems to be better. Emmy has really enjoyed getting out and about these past few weeks. She has had the opportunity to enjoy some awesome activities with great family and friends. She has had a wonderful summer. We are so thankful that God has allowed her to enjoy so many summer activities. She loved camping over Labor Day.

She has another UTI and her antibiotic makes her sick to her tummy daily, but this hasn't slowed her down.

She is out tonight in her car racing Jesse on his tractor. Jesse has the advantage. He weighs less, so his tractor goes faster than her car. We have decorated our house with lovely fall decorations. Emmy is excited for fall and Halloween. Then she can focus on Santa. Nothing like rushing winter.

I pray that she continues to do well so that she can enjoy her upcoming favorite holidays. With the help of a lot of people during this past year, we have tried to provide Emmy opportunities to celebrate her favorite holidays. It would be so wonderful for her to be able to celebrate on the actual holiday. We are so blessed. Every day is another miracle.

September 6, 2012

Fill up the gas tank - $65.00. A few groceries to make some sweets for my sweeties - $35.00. Racing home from work to share a beautiful rainbow with my beautiful best girl Emmy – PRICELESS! This is the first one she has gotten a chance to see this year. She is so excited and so sad when it goes away. We watch it in the sky until the very last second. "It's just another ordinary miracle today."

Thank you, God, for rainbows; especially ones that make little girls smile with excitement.

September 7, 2012

After Hospice consulted with the doctors it has been determined that, due to the progression of the tumor, Emmy now has a neurogenic bladder. The muscles are no longer allowing her bladder to empty as it should. This is causing an increase in bacteria in the bladder, which in turn is causing the chronic UTIs. The bad news is that Emmy will now have a permanent catheter, which she is NOT HAPPY about. She keeps telling me, "Mommy, me want it out, get it out now!" Can you blame her? The good news is that hopefully there will no longer be the chronic UTIs, which also means no more yucky antibiotics.

Emmy is uncomfortable today, but hopefully after twenty-four hours, her body will become used to the catheter, and she will no longer feel the constant urinating sensation that she currently feels. Tonight I am praying that Emmy is more comfortable and that she does not try to pull the catheter out. Looks like it will be a late night keeping watch.

WEEK TWENTY-NINE

September 12, 2012

Dear Dad,

Things have been crazy with Emmy the past couple days. Her sleep schedule is off so I am not getting much rest right now. She is becoming needier. She wants me with her every second she is awake so my only time to catch up on everything else (or write) is when she is sleeping. My employer has asked me to put in more hours per week if I can. I am exhausted, overwhelmed, and stressed. I have no idea how I am going to do all of this.

In all that we have gone through, I have never been angry. I couldn't be angry with anyone. I wasn't angry with God. I have faith that everything happens for a reason. My family has been through too much to believe any other way. God didn't make Emmy sick. I don't feel He would ever want her to go through what she is going through right now.

Mom's friend Barbara lost her son in a car accident when he was twenty-three years old. She shared her feelings with me and after listening to her, this is what I think. Parents have been losing their children since the beginning of time. Mary had to endure the loss of her son, Jesus; why should I be any different? We are all adoptive parents to our children. Our children are God's children first. We take care of them until He calls them home, some sooner than others. We all choose our path before we are born. Before Emmy was born, she agreed to accept this life and endure this disease. This was so she could <u>teach us and we could all learn something from her</u>.

I agreed to accept her into my life, to love and cherish her knowing that our time together would be short. Her biological brother, Jesse, was a bonus. God gave me Jesse so that I could see glimpses of Emmy through him, his personality, his mannerisms, and his smile. He really is so much like her. He is her "Minnie Me."

I have experienced many emotions though this: fear, confusion, sadness, stress, helplessness, joy, but not anger. I have questions. Am I doing the right thing by not telling Emmy that she is going to die? Have I been a good mother? If a miracle doesn't happen and Emmy doesn't live, is it because I haven't prayed enough or had enough faith? Have I made her happy? Has she enjoyed her life? Has she been able to do everything she wanted to? Have I prepared her for what will happen? How do I help my kids, my nieces, and my nephews deal with this loss? These are the things I think about.

My focus is on giving her as many fun experiences as possible for her to enjoy life, while at the same time planning for her death. I want her funeral to be a celebration of her life. This may seem bizarre to some, or may look like I do not have faith, but planning has been therapeutic, a stress reliever for me.

I am a planner. I need to know that I have done everything necessary. I plan now in case I can't plan later. I have no idea how I will be emotionally when the time comes for Emmy to graduate to receive her angel wings. I take comfort in knowing that I have done everything I can for her and for her funeral.

The majority of my stress revolves around Emmy's behaviors. How much she has changed. Her aggression, her need to have me with her at all times. I think this all stems from fear. She knows that something isn't right, but she isn't sure what it is. She doesn't have the language skills or insight to ask. She obsesses about being away from me.

We haven't told her what is happening to her for fear it will scare her. We have talked about heaven, and what a wonderful place it is. We have read *Heaven is for Real* to her. I have told her I can't wait to go to heaven. She can't understand why I would say that. She told me she didn't like Jesus. Heaven is a place people go and you will "Never, ever, ever, ever, ever see them again," as Emmy sees it. We talked about angels and how they take people to heaven. She told me she would be an angel so she could take me to heaven and we could be together forever.

I am very emotional tonight. Emmy is sleeping. I am going to rest now while I can.

*****

Bruce

I am fire-breathing, venom-spitting mad. Why is this happening to Emmy? Why does my daughter Tammy have to endure such horrific agony? How can a mother watch as her daughter journeys one day closer to a slow death, her body wasting away towards a skeleton with skin? Why can't I fix this? I can't understand what God's plan is out of all of this.

I storm back and forth across the rug in my man cave. "Maybe Tammy isn't mad at you but I am dang mad," I yell, shaking my fists at the ceiling at God. "Why did you call me in the middle of the night in 1995 into healing ministry?" This is not part of healing. This is disease. This goes against everything I believe in about healing in Scriptures.

Isaiah 55:8-9

> [8] For my thoughts are not your thoughts, neither are your ways my ways, declares the LORD. [9] For as the heavens are higher than the earth, so are my ways higher than your ways and my thoughts than your thoughts.

In June and July, Emmy's Facebook page members reached close to 11,000 people all over the world. People who had been out of touch with Jesus were now praying. Is this all about gathering the sheep?

My God is a loving God. My ministry is to lead people to an intimate relationship with the Fathering heart of God and to have an experiential encounter of His love. His love heals all. This doesn't feel like my Loving God. This doesn't seem like my Loving God. This doesn't appear to be a Loving God.

Romans 8:28-30

> [28] And we know that for those who love God all things work together for good for those who are called according to his purpose. (ESV)

This emotional rollercoaster is wearing me down. One day we are looking at death standing at the door and then the next day is another honeymoon period of reprieve.

Jesus, what are you up to? Is Emmy here to teach people about your love and mercy? Is her purpose to draw people to a closer relationship with you? Will she be the incentive for people to pray more and return to church? Is she your instrument to show people your love?

How sad that a little girl has to die in order for people to get a wakeup call about what is really important in their lives. That, in this materialistic prosperity-based culture, it takes an emotional train wreck to stop people in their tracks. That it takes a little four-year-old girl to show us how to love like Jesus. How to stop and smell the flowers. How to see beauty in all of God's creation. The joy of a butterfly flying through the air. The beauty of a rainbow bridging across the sky. The delight of a raindrop landing on a cheek. The smells, the sounds, and the sights all around us that we flippantly take for granted.

How can my loving God put a mother through so much pain and torment? What lens do I use to see His mercy in all of this? So many other children also are dying of brain stem cancer. All the research so far has not found a cure. Funding is scarce. Somehow, someway, Emmy's story will contribute towards the progress of a cure. This fire-breathing dragon must be stopped by the Sword of the Spirit. You despicable cancer, child-killing villain, you will be defeated. Amen.

OCTOBER

October 1, 2012

Emmy's disease is progressing. The honeymoon is over. Our house is so quiet. She is unable to speak now. What she does say is hard to understand. She isn't eating much and is having a hard time keeping food down. She is very weak and tired. It is hard for her to hold her head up if she is sitting. Outings are limited now and kept short. She still giggles, gets excited, and experiences joy in each day.

I was hoping she would be here for Christmas, but in these past couple of days, I am not sure that will happen. We have been blessed with so much extra time.

WEEK THIRTY-TWO

October 2, 2012

Tomorrow marks week thirty-two. Emmy does not seem to be in any discomfort from her neurogenic bladder. She is urinating daily and no longer requires additional pain medications. She has grown weaker and more tired. She usually naps a couple times during the day and sleeps most of the night. Her muscles have grown weaker.

Now that Emmy isn't talking anymore, our house seems so quiet. She makes noises that are extremely difficult to understand and her voice sounds very strained when she tries to communicate.

She is eating less and continues to occasionally vomit. She is having more difficulty swallowing. She eats only soft foods. We have had to thicken her drinks to keep her from choking and aspirating when she swallows. She has lost twenty-five pounds but feels heavier now since her body just hangs as I move her from bed to couch to bath, etc.

She is my hero. Emmy is so much stronger than I could ever hope to be. Through all of this, she continues to live, laugh, and love. We snuggle, giggle, and enjoy each other every day, hour, minute, second. We are so blessed to have been given more time than the doctors originally thought we had.

I am not ready to let her go if God chooses to take her home. There is so much she hasn't done yet. I see children walking to school and think about Emmy starting Kindergarten next fall. She will miss her preschool graduation, sixth grade graduation, first dance, first crush, first kiss, first love, high school graduation, college graduation, marriage, becoming a mother, a grandmother, and so much more. I try not to think about all of that, but as her disease progresses, and I see her change, it is sometimes hard to stay strong. I will continue to think about how blessed we are for the time we have and make the most of every second I have with this amazing little girl.

WEEK THIRTY-THREE

October 12, 2012

How Can I Help Her Say Good-Bye

We have reached the thirty-third week. Emmy has been uncomfortable from the UTI. We will collect another urine sample tomorrow to see if the antibiotic has cleared it up. If so, we will be able to start a long-term antibiotic to prevent any UTIs in the future.

Our biggest struggle this week is feeding. She is having a very difficult time opening her mouth wide enough to take in food. Her food and beverage intake has been minimal. She is only eating applesauce, yogurt, and ice cream—those foods that have a little substance but slide down her throat easily. The challenge has been getting her to keep in what she is eating. She has been unable to keep anything down the past four days. She is taking anti-nausea medication, but she is still nauseated.

She has lost twenty-seven pounds. It is a good thing that before this she was chunky. Emmy has always been pleasantly plump. She was the chubbiest baby I had ever seen. She looks so different now. Her cheeks are still full and round, but her legs, arms, and tummy are getting so thin. I think her brother Jesse's ham hock legs are bigger than Emmy's, now.

Earlier I mentioned about time and how we want time to pass to get to the things we enjoy, want it to stop in order to hold on to something, or want it to go back to a special memory or a time when things were better. I have been feeling all of these lately. I want time to pass to allow Emmy to enjoy the upcoming holidays she loves so much. I want time to stand still so that I can hold on to her forever. I want time to go back to the day when she wasn't sick. To a time when she could run, play with her friends, talk, laugh, smile, and enjoy foods that she loves. To a time when she could enjoy being a little girl with the hope of an amazing future.

As each day passes, I see the changes in her that show me her disease is progressing. *No child should ever have to live with such a horrible disease.* To have to live with pain, to live with confusion about what is happening, and fear of the unknown. *How can I help her say good-bye?* How can I prepare her for what is happening without causing her to be stressed, anxious, and/or afraid to leave us? How do you help your four-year-old understand that heaven is an amazing place where she will feel a love she has never felt before when all she wants is to be with her mommy, daddy, brothers, and the rest of her family and friends? With each passing day, I feel like she is slipping farther and farther away from me. Before I know it, she could be gone from here. I know in my heart that she will be in an amazing place, but it doesn't help me from already missing her. I pray that God will help me find a way to help her understand and to comfort her.

October 15, 2012

Emmy did eat a little applesauce today and she drank three containers of PediaSure®. She was very groggy, tired, and weak. She understands what we are saying to her and responds by shaking her head yes or no. She is exhausted. We were up the major part of last night. She wanted to drink nonstop. She never napped today. Her eyes would close, but she wouldn't give in to sleep. We are still up now. I have given her medications to help relax her, but she will not go to sleep. She is a fighter. I think that she has a sense of what is happening and she is afraid to close her eyes.

Her temperature is elevating again and she is back on oxygen. Her heart rate is extremely rapid. I pray that Emmy finds peace and that she is able to let herself go to sleep. She wants me in her bed beside her while she nestles up to me. I don't want her to be too warm because of my body heat, but she needs to have me close. To feel her mom's caress. To feel loved in her mom's arms. I wish I could do much more for her.

WEEK THIRTY-FOUR

October 16, 2012

Tomorrow marks week thirty-four. Emmy is fighting so hard. She is very weak and tired. She finally allowed herself to drift to sleep at two a.m. She is asleep and unresponsive to our voice or touch. Her little body is working so hard right now.

I spent the evening trying to control her elevated temperature. She has a rattling noise when she breathes. She is on oxygen and her level is at eighty-nine percent. Her heart rate is extremely rapid. As I sit here writing this, I keep thinking about how quiet my house is right now. The boys are at school and Emmy is resting peacefully. Brother Jesse insisted on blowing Emmy kisses before he left for daycare today. I think he senses something. Denny dropped him off and told me that this is the first time in a long time that Jesse fussed about going to daycare.

I have been hopeful that Emmy would get to wear her owl costume trick or treating. She has been looking forward to that. I also know how excited she has been that Santa would come see her. Now I feel like I missed my opportunity to do these things for her. It may be too late. If only I planned for them sooner. She could have been able to experience them one last time. As I am feeling all of these emotions, I just want her to be at comfort and at peace.

She looks so peaceful right now. Denny is reading some of Emmy's favorite stories to her. I don't want her to wake up if it means she will have to experience any more discomfort or fear. She was so afraid to let herself fall asleep last night. She fought it with everything she had. She stared at me so intently as if she felt it was the last time she would see me. I want her not to be afraid to take this next step in her journey.

I have told her heaven is amazing. I have told her when she gets there everything will be okay. She will feel better without any more pain or fear. She will be able to talk, run, and play. I have told her that it is okay to go and that before she can turn around, Mommy and Daddy will be right behind her. I pray that she understands. I pray that Emmy can take the next step in her journey without fear or reservation and that she will run to the abundance of love that awaits her. God does hold her in the palm of His hand.

October 16, 2012 Evening

Emmy continues to sleep. She did not wake today. I don't know if she will awake or if she is now in a coma. She continues to be unresponsive. She does flutter her eyes from time to time. I know that she can hear everything we are saying. She is so peaceful.

The rattling when she breathes has disappeared and her heart rate has decreased. Her little body does not appear to be working so hard to get oxygen. The calmness and stillness in her body comforts me, knowing that she is not in any pain. She looks like an angel as she sleeps.

I am thankful to family and friends who stop by today for a visit. Their love and support mean so much to us and to Emmy. She loves having company and I know she can feel their presence.

I am thankful to everyone for all the kind words, thoughts, and prayers. I am in awe of the amount of messages and comments I receive today. I pray that as Emmy continues on this journey to heaven, she remains as peaceful as she is right now. Tonight we will all try to get some rest.

October 17, 2012

Emmy wakes and stays awake today until around twelve p.m. She is able to take in liquids and her PediaSure® through a medicine dropper. Her temperature remains normal throughout the day. She does not experience any discomfort or any headaches. She naps until two-thirty p.m. She is so thirsty and hungry when she wakes. We can't get her PediaSure® into her fast enough. Through the medicine dropper she drinks two bottles of PediaSure®, water, a small bowl of potato soup, and some applesauce. I wait for her little tummy to explode since she hasn't eaten much for a few days.

Her body is just so tired and weak. She has been through so much. She is unable to hold her head up. She can't hold her sippy cup and bring it to her mouth without assistance. She responds to questions by shaking her head and eye movements, but the movements are very subtle. Her body is very limp when I pick her up.

Even with these limitations, she is feisty. She insists on doing her cup on her own. When I try to help, she pulls it away. When I ask if she wants to do it on her own, she shakes her head yes. She still bosses me without saying a word. She points her finger to change the TV station, points at the bed or couch to tell me where to sit, uses sign language to tell me she wants to eat or drink. I love that I am able to do all these things for her.

October 18, 2012

Emmy has been awake since two-thirty a.m. She has been drinking milk and PediaSure®. She eats half of a mashed banana with some milk to make a consistency able to fit in the medicine dropper. Unlike yesterday, she is able to lift her sippy cup to her mouth by herself today. She is very excited about that. She wants to be so independent. Her coloring looks good. Her temp is normal. Her only discomfort is in her tummy which I think is caused by the fiber in the PediaSure®. The Pepcid® AC she took seemed to help. Her heart rate is a little lower than it has been, which is good. She is very comfortable.

Her muscles are weak. She is unable to support her head when she sits upright. She enjoys watching one of her favorite cartoons, *Max and Ruby*. She is starting to get a bit drowsy. I hope that she will drift to sleep for a little while. I talk to her about the holiday festivities planned for her this weekend. She is very excited about the activities and the visitors coming to see her. We are so thankful for another day.

October 20, 2012

What a day. We are having the best time. Many people come out to celebrate Emmy's holiday extravaganza and help us create some very special memories. She loves it. We couldn't have asked for a better day. It is wonderful to meet so many people. Emmy really enjoys passing out the candy, but her favorite part is Santa. She would stay in his lap all day if we let her. She has had a very big day and is now fast asleep with her new furry friends.

I am thankful to Helping Hands, Cambridge Springs Fire Department, Craig Newell Welding, and Santa for all the gifts. We are overwhelmed. They created a day we will never forget. Emmy and the boys love all their toys. I am in awe of the love and support that has been shown towards my family. I am so thankful for caring so deeply about our special little girl.

October 23, 2012

Emmy starts this morning with a temperature. She sleeps on and off throughout the day and wakes several times through the night. Yesterday she experienced some discomfort from her neurogenic bladder. She has urinary retention, which in turn can cause bladder spasms. I believe the discomfort she experiences is from the bladder spasms. It seems to cause her the most discomfort right after she urinates. She continues to take the antibiotic to prevent her from getting any more UTIs. I hope the medication helps her rest comfortably.

WEEK THIRTY-FIVE

October 24, 2012

Emmy has been tired, but pain free. We have a wonderful surprise today. Denny's cousins Jessica Slayton and Michelle Wilmoth stop by for a visit. Jessica said she and a friend of hers, Dave, want to do something for Emmy and our family. She asks if it would be okay if we receive a delivery. I say "Sure."

Right at that time, in pulls a van from Treasured Memories. How nice, I think, Emmy will love to have some flowers and more balloons. Lois from Treasured Memories comes to the door and says, "Where do you want me to put the things?"

"On the table," I reply. "What do you mean, things?" I ask. In she comes with package after package after package.

There are balloons and flowers. There are gift baskets with fruit, candy, meat and cheese, pasta, salad, ice cream fixings, ice cream, cereal, applesauce, pudding, toys, coloring books, bubbles, stuffed animals, and the list goes on and on. Did I mention toys? There is a card attached that reads, "Every day is full of surprises!" Yes, it is, and this is a huge surprise.

Emmy is asleep on her bed with all of her balloons. As I look at her an image keeps popping into my head from the movie *Up*. Her bed has so many balloons it looks as though it could fly away. I have said it before and I'll say it again. The generosity and love that has been shown to Emmy and my family is overwhelming.

October 27, 2012

First, I want to take this moment to tell you all how much I appreciate my husband, Denny. I just haven't written enough about him and what he does for us.

He stays home Tuesdays and Thursdays to care for Emmy, while I do Mondays, Wednesdays, and Fridays. Emmy is definitely a Mama's girl right now. If I am home, she always wants me to help her instead of her dad. I know this is hard for Denny, but he doesn't let it get him down. He doesn't push himself on Emmy. He lets her decide when she is ready for Daddy time because he cares more about making her happy than how he feels when she pushes him away. While I am caring for Emmy, he is doing all the other nightly things in our home, like grocery shopping, cleaning the supper dishes, bathing the boys, making sure homework is done, getting bedtime snacks, reading bedtime stories and snuggling with Jesse until he falls asleep. All of this can be very stressful. Jesse can be a challenge, especially now as he engages in attention-seeking behaviors. He is struggling with all of the changes, as are the rest of us.

As I said, I haven't really mentioned much about Denny. I think men often express themselves differently than women. We are more likely to wear our hearts on our sleeves. Many women are talkers. We like to talk about everything, whereas men often keep things inside. They don't like to talk about how they are feeling. We all have our own coping mechanisms that help us deal with difficult situations.

I comment on Facebook about Emmy. Writing about what is happening in our family is therapeutic for me. I have mentioned the boys and how they are dealing with all of this. Jesse is still so young and death is so abstract for JP to understand, due to his autism.

Emmy is such a little fighter. She is tired, weak and worn, but she is still fighting. Eating and drinking become increasingly difficult for her. She isn't getting much nourishment. When she asks to eat, she takes in very small amounts to make her satisfied. When I look into her eyes, I feel like there are so many questions she has for me, but is unable to ask. I wish I knew what she was thinking.

She responds to yes and no questions with eye movements now. Her head isn't moving much anymore. She is just so very weak.

I am certain I would not be able to remain strong without Denny, the love and support from our family and friends, and faith that God will take care of all of us.

We will continue to help Emmy to experience and truly live every day to its fullest.

October 28, 2012

I Fear Her Fight Is Starting to Dwindle

Emmy is asleep after her bath tonight. That always seems to tire her out more. She usually goes to sleep right after her bath. She looks so tiny and frail when I bathe her. I could feel all the bones in her back and rib area when I remove her shirt. She used to be so plump and now her tummy is so thin. She is down to forty-five pounds.

She has taken in some water today. She drank two sips of a root beer float. She had two bites of applesauce and one bite of mashed potatoes. She isn't interested in eating much, but wants to drink all the time. I think she likes the sensation of the cool wet water in her mouth. At least half of what she takes into her mouth seeps out the sides. I can't see how she can sustain life much longer on her food intake. Only by the grace of God.

She is very weak and tired. Things that she used to fight me about she isn't fighting anymore. It used to be a struggle to get her to take her meds, but now she just lies there and lets me give them to her. She has been such a fighter through all of this, but I fear her fight is starting to dwindle.

Tonight, she is resting peacefully. For this, I am so very thankful.

October 30, 2012

Emmy wakes today at five a.m. but is now asleep for a nap. She is still taking in minimal food, but she seems to be drinking more. Hospice brings us a feeding syringe which is bigger than a medicine syringe. I hope that that will work better as long as I can get it between her clenched teeth. For as weak as she is, her jaws are incredibly strong.

We read some stories today. She wants to look through her baby book. We look through all the pages and her photo albums while I talk about what is happening in each of the pictures. She loves to look at pictures of herself when she was little. My talking seems to lull her to sleep. I won't take offense. I am going to assume she is just that tired and not that I am just that boring.

She is comfortable and does not exhibit any signs of pain. Even though she is tired and weak, she seems more calm and at peace than she has in the past. She looks like an angel.

We are taking it one day at a time and treasuring every moment with Emmy.

NOVEMBER

WEEK THIRTY-SIX

November 1, 2012

What does a parent think about when she is bathing her lethargic, limp, lifeless like child while the child's big brown eyes are looking at her? All the parent can see is sadness, confusion, fear, and uncertainty. This is what I am thinking: what a terrible, horrible disease. Why should anyone ever have to endure any of this? How is it possible that with all of today's scientific technology a doctor can tell you that your child has a disease and there is nothing that can be done? No matter what treatments you try, or don't try, there is only one outcome. *HOW IS THIS POSSIBLE?*

I miss the spunk. I miss the sassiness. I miss the strong-willed determination. I even miss the tantrums. Yes, her tantrums. I miss her smile. I miss her giggle. I miss the hugs and kisses. I miss her voice.

Through all of this, Emmy has always remained alert to her surroundings. I have recently noticed times where she stares off into the distance in an almost unresponsive state. I feel like with every passing moment *SHE IS SLIPPING FARTHER AND FARTHER AWAY FROM US.*

I Miss My Baby Girl

We are at thirty-six weeks and counting. She appears to be comfortable and free from any pain. Our biggest challenge continues to be with feeding. She doesn't appear to be hungry, but enjoys the stimulation of foods and beverages in her mouth. She really isn't taking much in, but likes the constant feel of something in her mouth. We continually provide her with liquids and pureed foods to satisfy her wants. This too helps make her comfortable. She remains very weak and tired. *How long can she last?*

I have been told that a million years here on Earth are captured in just one second in heaven, illustrating the concept of timelessness. I know and believe that when God chooses to take Emmy home it won't be *"good-bye,"* it will be *"I love you and I'll miss you, but I will see you later."* Within a blink of an eye we will all be together in heaven. She won't even have the chance to realize we were apart. It is those of us left behind who will feel the separation is like an eternity.

I am so very thankful for time and even more thankful that she is comfortable and at peace. I am praying that through whatever the next step is for Emmy on this journey, she will always be at peace.

November 2, 2012

I wake today to a cold, dark, damp, dreary day, and then the magic happens. For a brief moment, the wet dampness turns to the most beautiful big white flakes of lace falling from the sky. I am privileged to witness the excitement in a little girl's big brown eyes when she sees her first snowfall of the year. Simply breathtaking. Emmy enjoys seeing the snow. It starts to come down a bit harder just before lunch. I hold her in my arms while we sing and twirl in the falling snow. She loves the feel of the cold soft flakes on her warm nose and eyelashes. Simple things can give such great pleasure. It is just another ordinary miracle today. I pray that there are many more simple things for Emmy to enjoy.

Thank you, God, for snow. Today has been a good day.

November 3, 2012

I Never Want to Forget!!!!

The house seems quiet and still. Sometimes in the still of the night, I find myself waking up to Emmy's voice. I look over at her, but she is fast asleep. I think to myself, it must have been a dream, but it felt so real. I feel like I am already forgetting what her little voice sounds like. I feel the need to go through home videos so I can hear her voice again. I am so thankful we have videos, pictures, and

Facebook posts. These things are all so precious to me now. I know I will always be able to use them to help me remember. I never want to forget a thing.

We have a toasty warm fire in the fireplace. I love to listen to the gentle crackling from the burning logs and watch the flaming colors glow. The smell brings back memories of my childhood, a cozy warm time when everything felt safe. Emmy loves the fire too. She wants us to build another one tonight.

She used to gain my attention with words or noises, but those have faded to faint groans. She also would use her right arm for sign language when she wanted to eat or drink. She seems to be unable to move her arms as she used to, making it difficult for her to use sign language. She used to lift her right leg into the air and slam it onto the bed when she really wanted my attention or wanted to wake me up. We have always called it her flipper foot, because, in the summer when she would swim in the pool, she would forcefully slam it down, similar to a whale in the water. She hasn't used her flipper foot in a week or so. Her head movement is minimal. She does answer yes and no questions through eye movement. I am thankful she remains responsive and uses her eyes as a way to communicate her needs to us.

The Lord's peace is upon her!

I have noticed some changes with Emmy over this past week. She has been sleeping through the night, which is a good thing. She usually takes two naps during the day. The increase in her sleeping is the progression of the disease. I like to attribute it to her being comfortable and at peace. She can now relax so she can rest. I am so very thankful for her continued comfort and peace. My prayers are that this continues throughout her journey. We will continue to find joy and happiness in the little things and cherish every moment we are blessed to have Emmy in our lives.

November 4, 2012

Thank You, Lord. Every day is another miracle!

I sat last night staring at Emmy, watching her sleep. She was so quiet, peaceful, and still. I thanked God for all of the gifts in my life and for the privilege to spend another day with such an extraordinary little girl. She is one of the best things that has ever happened in my life. I prayed for the opportunity to spend even just another moment with her. I fell asleep with ease knowing she was resting comfortably without pain.

I wake to the pitter-patter of little feet coming down the stairs. Jesse is calling "Mama" as he searches for me. He climbs on the couch to snuggle, but not for long. He hops up and runs to his Sissy to give her a big, huge, good morning kiss.

"Gentle, Jesse. Please be careful not to wake Emmy. She needs her rest," I say. He climbs on her bed ever so carefully, placing the gentlest kiss on her cheek. My heart melts.

I am watching, waiting, and wondering if her eyes will open. They do not. My eyes begin to swell with tears. I wonder if last night was the final time on this Earthly World I would have the chance to see my baby girl's beautiful big brown eyes. I patiently sit, waiting, waiting, waiting for the slightest movement. I am afraid to wake her for fear she will not wake up. I just sit here, still, watching her sleep. Then I notice the blanket move ever so slightly. She is beginning to stir. Her sparkling eyes stare into mine. I pray, "Thank you, God, for another day."

Emmy is into another honeymoon phase of her disease and is doing better today with swallowing. So far today, she has been able to drink fifteen to eighteen ounces of milk through the medicine syringe. She also drank half a bottle of chocolate PediaSure®. Emmy wants to get out of the house today. We are going for a car ride a little later. I am so thankful Emmy will have the opportunity to get outside to enjoy another wonderful autumn day. I am certain she will fall asleep. Can you blame her? I love to sleep in the car too. I pray tomorrow brings her as much joy as today.

WEEK THIRTY-SEVEN

November 9, 2012

We have reached thirty-seven weeks. It is hard for me to write how Emmy is doing. It changes so much from day to day. Yesterday was a difficult day for Emmy. She again was not able to swallow anything. Everything I put in her mouth with the medicine syringe came back out and ran down her face. I saw she was getting frustrated. It broke my heart to watch her try so hard and not be able to swallow. Her eyes showed an expression of concern. She looked confused about why she wasn't able to swallow. It was hard to watch her and know I couldn't help her.

Today Emmy spends the entire day with her Daddy. Daddy reads her stories and snuggles with her in her bed. I would have loved to have taken a picture of that. Denny has to squeeze himself in the bed to fit. He says to keep from falling out he has to hold on to the rail on the opposite side of the bed. Oh, the sacrifices we make for our children. I am sure Emmy loves every minute of it.

I have to go to work today. After I get home, I feed Emmy. She is able to swallow her milk and eggnog without difficulties. She does love her eggnog. I can't feed her fast enough. Before swallowing one bite, I feel her little hand batting at my arm to signal she wants more. She eats, gets a bath, and drifts off to sleep. She has been resting so comfortably, sleeping through the night.

The uncertainty of what tomorrow will bring is so hard. This really has been an emotional roller coaster. There are so many ups and downs. One minute I wonder if Emmy will still be with us for Thanksgiving and then next I think maybe she will be still be here at Christmas time. She is so full of surprises.

God is full of surprises

Every day is full of surprises. We had made our reservation for Emmy to visit Santa in the Woods for December 9. Yesterday, I had a surprise phone call. Sam Hawley from Holly Hills called me to ask if he could take our family on our ride sooner than December 9. He wanted to be sure Emmy got a chance to experience Santa in the Woods one more time. It was all I could do to fight back tears of joy.

The Hawleys are a very special family. We are so thankful for everything they have done for us. We already have plans for this weekend. We are hoping we will be able to take our ride either the seventeenth or eighteenth of November. We are waiting for a confirmation of when Santa will be able to come.

I tell Emmy about my phone call with Sam. She is so excited about this year's ride. She wants to watch the video from last Christmas of her driving the horses. We also watch the video of our ride last February after Emmy's diagnosis. She gets a kick out of watching it.

We are taking it one day at a time. We find the joy in every day and cherish every moment.

November 12, 2012

Beautiful Blustery Breeze.

Dancing Though the Trees.

That is what we wake to this morning. The sun is shining so bright. The temperature is warm. I ask Emmy if she wants to go outside. She expresses "yes" in the special way she does. Her eyes are so big and bright with excitement. I carry Emmy to the front porch swing. Cradling her in my arms, we slowly swing back and forth while gazing into each other's eyes.

We then close our eyes and listen to the sounds surrounding us. Taking it all in. Soaking in precious memories. The wind blows gently. The leaves begin to rustle. I hear the wind growing stronger. A gust blows. The leaves swish through the air. Under the tone of the rustling leaves, I hear the sound the whisking wind causes when the soft tinkling of wind chimes play their methodical songs in the distance.

I feel a tickling on my cheek as warm air blows ever so gently through my hair. We sit quietly, listening, feeling, soaking in the beauty of the moment. Wishing it would never end. It is surely a beautiful blustery breeze.

The expression in her eyes can tell you a story without saying a word. They are the opening to her heart. You can't help but feel overcome with love when you stare deeply into the soul of her heart.

*****

Emmy wants to eat when she wakes at six a.m. She has a little difficulty swallowing. I don't want to give her too much at once after yesterday's sickness, so I limit her intake. By seven-thirty, she is ready to eat again. This time swallowing is easier and she is able to finish her milk. Emmy's oxygen levels are low so we keep her on the oxygen machine all day. She has a slight temperature this morning, but after medication, it returns to normal and stays at normal the rest of the day. Emmy is able to swallow her milk at lunch and dinner without much difficulty. She never gets sick today.

Emmy takes a nap after lunch. I tell her someone very special is coming to see us after supper. I remind her Santa is coming to visit. Her smile isn't visible on the outside, but I can tell she is grinning from ear to ear on the inside.

After dinner we all change clothes for our pictures with Santa. We sit in the living room watching one of Emmy's favorite cartoons when we hear the jingling of bells and a "Ho Ho Ho!" from the front porch. I check and, sure enough, Santa is at my door. I invite him into our home. He comes into the living room to visit with Emmy. She wants to sit on his lap. Santa passes out presents.

I return Emmy to her bed where Santa comes to tell her good-bye. It is time for Santa to go, but first he gives Emmy a very special gift. Santa gives Emmy the Jingle Bells the reindeer wear when traveling on Christmas Eve. It doesn't take long for Jesse to acquire the bells. They are now hanging on our door. Santa says his final good-byes and a "Ho Ho Ho, Merry Christmas!" as he walks out the door, but not before I give him a great big hug.

It is a very special day for all of us. We created many special memories. Saturday we will get the opportunity to create many more. Tonight I am praying that Emmy will breathe better tomorrow. My hope is that by Saturday, she will no longer need to be on the oxygen machine to assist her breathing.

WEEK THIRTY EIGHT

November 14, 2012

It is just after midnight. This is the second night in a row Emmy wakes and wants to eat. It only takes her about a half-hour to eat. She does a great job swallowing without any coughing or choking.

I scoop her into my arms and carry her to the rocking chair. Oh, how I have missed rocking my baby girl. I sit cradling her like a baby as we rock back and forth while watching the warm glow of red and orange hot embers in the fireplace. She drifts off to sleep while I sing her favorite lullaby, "Baby Mine." I used to sing this lullaby to her every night when she was a baby. It is from the Disney movie *Dumbo*. The circus men lock Mrs. Jumbo up away from her baby, Dumbo, because they all think she has gone mad. She is the gentlest elephant and only becomes what they call "mad" when she is protecting her baby. Isn't this what any mother does when she protects her baby? Don't we all get a little upset or angry when we think someone is trying to harm our little ones? As mothers, don't we do all we can to keep our babies safe?

Dumbo is heartbroken because he is away from his mommy. Timothy Mouse takes Dumbo to see his mother. The circus men locked Mrs. Jumbo in shackles and she can't reach the window to see her baby through the iron bars. She extends her trunk through the bars reaching to find Dumbo. She can't see him, but she feels him with every fiber of her being, softly caressing his head with her trunk. As big tears drop from Dumbo's eyes, Mrs. Jumbo scoops up her baby, cradling him, rocking him ever so gently in her loving trunk while singing "Baby Mine." It is a very touching song. It perfectly displays a mother's unconditional love for her baby and how hard it is for them to be away from each other.

I rock back and forth with my eyes closed singing this very special lullaby to Emmy while she lays sleeping in my arms. It is a perfect moment in time, and I wish it could last forever, knowing when I no longer can see my baby I will still feel her with every fiber of my being.

She will "lay her head close to my heart, never to part, baby of mine."

Another incredible memory.

November 16, 2012

So quiet. I lay in my bed at night listening, waiting, afraid to fall asleep for fear I won't hear Emmy. Her voice is so quiet now. She makes the softest whimper when she needs something from me. If I don't listen closely, I may miss it.

The past few nights Emmy has been waking more than usual. She has wanted something to eat so I feed her and she goes back to sleep. Last night was different. I kept waking to the faintest murmur. I looked over at Emmy. She was staring at me while making the quietest moaning noises. "Emmy, what is wrong"? I asked. I ran through the usual yes/no questions. Do you want something to eat? Does anything hurt? Do you need to potty? Does your tummy hurt? Do you want me to put on your cartoons? With every question I asked I got the same gesture from Emmy: "No." I could tell by looking into her eyes she needed something from me. She wanted something I had not given her yet. After about twenty minutes of questions, I finally realized what she needed. "Emmy, do you want Mommy to climb in bed with you?" I asked. Her big brown eyes moved up and down to indicate "yes." The expression on her face jumped out at me as if to say, "Yes, Mommy, you finally guessed it. It's about time."

I climbed in her twin bed next to her. I had to slide her over to make room since she barricaded herself with so many toys and stuffed animals. I sat listening to her breathe, feeling the warmth of her little body as she snuggled in next to me. Within seconds she was asleep. While she was fast asleep, I climbed out of her bed and back into mine. When I was just about asleep, I would hear a noise. Somehow she always knew I wasn't beside her anymore. I crawled back into her bed until she was fast asleep again. This went on several more times throughout the night. I finally gave in and said, "You win, Emmy. Mommy will sleep with you tonight." Sometimes the comfort of a warm loving touch is all we need to make us feel safe. Emmy slept peacefully, safe in her mother's arms.

Emmy has not vomited since last Sunday. She has not been in any pain or discomfort. The tubing we are using for feedings is working great. She is getting much more into her mouth and it makes swallowing easier too. She does tire very easily. She has been taking an average of three naps per day in addition to her night sleeping. If I were smart, I would nap when she naps but I always seem to find some tasks that need to be completed. I get that from my dad.

Tomorrow is our big day. We are going for our Santa in the Woods ride at Holly Hill Farms. Emmy is looking forward to it. She says she wants to drive the horses and sit on Santa's lap.

November 17, 2012

When we wake this morning, I tell Emmy today is the day we are going to see Santa at the Cabin in the Woods. She takes a deep breath in, shakes her arms, and her big brown eyes open wider. Her facial expressions and body language scream, "Yeah, Yeah, Yeah!"

"Emmy, do you want to drive the horses?" I ask. Her eyes move in a definite "yes" motion. We all get ready, go out the door, and go on our big adventure.

We pull into Holly Hill Belgians at ten-thirty a.m. The large brown covered wagon is hooked to the two large Belgian horses. They are ready to take us on our ride. We get out of the car. The first noise I hear is the ringing sleigh bells attached to the horses. The sky is blue and the sun so bright. There isn't any snow. But that is alright. The air is a little cool, but the sun makes it feel warm. Warm enough to wear a sweater and a light coat. Emmy wants to visit the horses first. After we introduce ourselves to the horses, we load onto the wagon. We are on the long trail leading to the Cabin in the Woods. One by one, all of the kids have the opportunity to drive the horses. Emmy is the last to drive. She drives them right up to the cabin where we all hope Santa is waiting inside

About halfway to the cabin we spot deer. They start running in the same direction as the wagon. We watch them in all their beauty, leaping with their white bushy tails behind them. They stop for a moment then start running again. We watch them until they cross the path before us. Then they disappear into the thick of the woods.

We gather on the front porch of the cabin. The door opens and inside I hear, "Ho Ho Ho." Sitting inside in his chair, waiting for us, is none other than Santa. Each of the children have the opportunity to sit on Santa's lap and receive a gift. I ask Emmy if she is ready to see Santa. Her eyes again motion a definite "yes." I gently place her in Santa's arms. She snuggles right in to his shoulder. He holds her so lovingly while he kisses her forehead. They look so comfortable sitting together. I think she would fall asleep in his arms if I leave her there for much longer. We all enjoy each other's company while eating doughnuts and drinking the yummiest hot cocoa ever. Santa must have some sort of secret ingredient to make it taste so good. We say our thank you's and good-byes. Then we load back on the wagon for our return ride.

In the barn we visit some new horses. The horse Big Mike is no longer at the Hawley's Holly Hill Belgians. He is now in Colorado pulling sleighs for other families. Emmy misses her "buddy," but enjoys making new friends. Their Belgian horses are beautiful animals. Their eyes are so big and brown and have so much expression. They too seem to tell a story just like Emmy's eyes.

It is a very special day. When we took this ride last March, never in my wildest dreams did I think Emmy would still be with us doing it again in November. This day we will all remember and hold dear to our hearts.

WEEK THIRTY NINE

November 21, 2012

What a difference a year can make. Last year at this time, we were unaware of the devastation that was going to happen to our family. We gathered together with family and celebrated Thanksgiving. Did I think about what I was thankful for—what I was really thankful for? At the time, I thought I did, but now I am not so sure. Many times significant things happen to us that make us look at life differently. For some it may be wonderful things like marriage, birth, adoption of a child, or retirement. For others it may be something tragic like an accident, loss of employment, or death of a loved one. For me it was a terrible diagnosis of a terminal illness for my beautiful little girl.

I am so thankful for my family and friends, including my Facebook family. The love and support shown towards my family is one of the things that help us to get through each day. I am so thankful for the gift of time. God has given us much more time with Emmy than we ever imagined we would have since the doctors diagnosed her last February. The six to eight weeks we initially thought we had has now turned into thirty-nine weeks and still counting. Last February, I didn't know if we would get the chance to celebrate any more holidays with Emmy. Easter came, and then her birthday, then Fourth of July, then Halloween, now Thanksgiving, and hopefully next will be Christmas.

November 24, 2012

Last night the neighbor's houses were all decorated for Christmas. Emmy and I were so excited. We went from window to window to see the beautiful brilliant colors from lights that glowed through the darkness. We talked about Christmas coming. We talked about Santa. We talked about making reindeer food to sprinkle out around our house so Santa would find us. We talked about putting out Christmas cookies for Santa. We talked about celebrating the birth of Baby Jesus. I prayed that Emmy would be here to enjoy all the beauty that Christmas brings.

We wake today to a beautiful white blanket of snow shimmering in the light. I sit Emmy up so she can see across our living room out through the back sliding glass doors. Her arms shake with excitement while her eyes keep moving up and down saying, "Yes! Yes!"

Thank you, God, for the beautiful white blanket of shimmering snow.

While feeding her this morning, I keep thinking back to when Emmy was an infant. She would always be so alert and wide awake, anxiously waiting for her bottle. After she was about halfway through her bottle she would start to fall asleep, all snug in my arms. I used to have to tickle her feet to wake her enough to finish her bottle. She does the same thing now.

She looks at me with her big brown eyes, so trusting, relying and depending on me to take care of her every want and need, feed her, change her, bathe her, cuddle her, and love her. She is wide-awake while she waits for me to get her food. Then she drifts off to sleep about halfway through, all cozy in her bed while I snuggle next to her. I have to keep calling her name to wake her so she can finish.

She is asleep more than she is awake now. Feedings, changings and baths seem to exhaust her. She tires easily. She is weak and frail. With all of this, she never complains.

Jesse likes to be near when I am feeding Emmy. He usually plays with his toys on the end of Emmy's table. Today he plays with his

Legos®. After he creates a masterpiece, he keeps saying over and over, "*Emmy, look. Look, Emmy, look.*"

Emmy is unable to turn her head to look. Even after turning her head in the right direction, her eyes appear to stare blankly into the distance. It is so hard to tell if she is focusing or staring through you. Jesse so badly wants his sister to look at what he has made. He wants her to acknowledge his creation. He wants an affirmation from her that she is listening to him. He wants her to pay attention to him. He wants his big sister. The big sister who plays with him. The big sister who kisses his boo boos when he gets hurt. The big sister who helps feed him when he asks her to. The big sister who brushes his hair. The big sister who always makes sure he has some of whatever she has. The big sister who comforts him when mommy or daddy scold him. He wants his big sister, the way she used to be.

Sometimes it breaks my heart to see them interact together. They have a very special bond. I wonder how Jesse will deal with all of this in the end. How will he be able to live without her? Will he look for her? Will he call for her? Will he ask for her? Will JP do the same? JP is the best big brother, but he won't ever be able to fill the shoes of Jesse's big sister. There will always be a hole, a void, an emotional wound. It will always feel like something is missing in our lives.

The boys may not fully understand what is happening; I know they sense something is wrong. I pray that we are able to fill our hearts with special memories. When Emmy passes on to be with Jesus, I pray these special memories will last until we are all together again. Until then, we will continue to cherish every day, hour, minute, and second Emmy blesses our lives.

November 25, 2012

The snow fell through the night and stuck to the ground. Today we wake to big beautiful flakes falling from the sky. There is enough snow to play in outside. I ask Emmy if she wants to go out and make snow angels. She gives me a definite "Yes! Yes!" over and over again. I haven't seen her so excited in a while. She keeps shaking her arms and her eyes are huge. She takes in a deep breath and makes her mouth into a partial smile. It is beautiful. She is glowing.

She acts as if she wants to say something. Jesse says it for her. He runs around inside the house shouting, "Yeah! Yeah!" We all get bundled up and head out into the cool crisp air. I help Emmy make her first snow angel of the year. After we finish I ask Emmy if she is ready to go back inside. She gives me a definite "No! No!" She loves being outside enjoying the beautiful snow.

Thank you, God, for the opportunity to create more special memories.

WEEK FORTY

November 27, 2012

When?

I am so thankful for every day God allows Emmy to continue to bless our lives. Tomorrow ends the fortieth week since diagnosis. As the holidays approach, I can't help but ask myself the question, "When?" When is He going to call her home? Will she be with us to celebrate Jesse's third birthday on December 15? Will we lose her December 22, the same day we lost a previous foster child who returned to his birth parents just three days before Christmas after we had raised him for the first two years of his life? Will she be here to celebrate Christmas?

Christmas is a joyous holiday full of hope and love. A time when we celebrate the birth of Jesus. The miracle child who was born of the Blessed Virgin Mary for us so He could one day die on the cross to take away our sins so those that believe in Him could have eternal life. It is during this most joyous holiday that I want to be able to concentrate on the miracle of birth. I want to be able to think about *Birth* and not think about *Death*. I want to be able to erase the question, "When?" from the back of my mind. I want to be able to focus on the here and now and not on what and when the future may hold.

I know when God chooses to take Emmy home there will be great sorrow, but there will also be great joy. There will be reason to celebrate because my little girl is guaranteed a place in heaven. I take comfort in knowing that because of the great sacrifice God made not sparing His only Son, I too will be able to one day see my little girl in heaven.

We will continue to cherish every day God blesses our family with Emmy. We are thankful to Him for the gifts He has given.

November 28, 2012

We have had a busy morning this first day of week forty-one. Today Emmy decides she wants to go for a swim. My little bathing beauty hasn't been in the hot tub since summer. We relax in the hot tub for about twenty minutes. She loves floating on her back and the feeling of weightlessness in her body. It takes some convincing to get her out. We get baths and do the rest of our morning routine.

Floating in the hot tub is hard work and it makes you hungry. Emmy is ready to eat again. Emmy keeps falling asleep during her feeding. I tell her I am going to have to tickle her feet to wake her up as I did when she was a baby during her bottles. She gets a kick out of that.

I put Emmy on the couch while I clean up from her feeding. When I come back into the living room, she is fast asleep. I am so glad we had the opportunity to share this special time together today.

November 30, 2012

We have a wonderful evening tonight. It is the annual tree lighting ceremony in Cambridge Springs. The weather is beautiful. All of the festivities take place outside in the park this year. It is awesome to see the community come together.

Emmy is so excited she is going to see Santa again. The festival begins with a beautiful song and a prayer. Next, Cambridge Springs Royalty Choir leads the community in singing Christmas carols while we all anxiously awaited the arrival of Santa. The park gets dark.

Then with the flip of one switch, it turns into a magical wonderland. Brilliant red, blue, green, yellow, and orange lights lit the gazebo. There is a white sign lit up that says, "North Pole." Santa's big chair is in the front of the gazebo. In the middle of the gazebo behind Santa's chair stands a beautifully decorated Christmas tree. So many lights cover the tree that it lights up the park. Everyone stares in amazement. The faint sound of a fire siren echoes in the distance. The kids all know a fire siren can only mean one thing. Santa is coming

The siren grows louder and louder as the fire truck draws closer and closer. The children's eyes grow bigger and bigger with the anticipation of Santa's arrival. In the storefront windows, you can see the reflection of the fire truck lights as it drives towards the park. Then, there it is in all its beauty. A big beautiful red shiny fire truck drives around the park with none other than St. Nicholas as a passenger. The children are mesmerized. They can't take their eyes off Santa. They watch as the fire truck rounded the end of the park and came to a halt. The air brakes let out a long hiss. The first thing you see is Santa's head looking out the window. The door swings open and Santa climbs out of the fire truck. His beard is whiter than snow. He keeps saying, "Ho Ho Ho!"

The children become more and more excited as Santa approaches the park. He heads our way. Oh my, he is coming right towards us. The excitement grows bigger and bigger. He stops right beside us and says, "Emmy, how are you, pumpkin? Merry Christmas." It feels just like the moment in the movie *Polar Express* when Santa announces the child who would receive the first gift of Christmas. Emmy is that child. Santa talks with Emmy for a few minutes, tells her he worries about her, gently kisses her forehead then heads to his big chair in front of the gazebo to greet the other children who had already began forming a line. The whole experience is simply magical.

DECEMBER

December 1, 2012

Emmy is so determined and such a little fighter. She seems to have a bit of her fight back this past week. I see glimpses of the old Emmy.

She is eating her liquid diet through the tubing and medicine syringe with ease. She takes in about fifteen to twenty ounces of Ensure® per day. She remains on a daily antibiotic to prevent any more UTIs. Emmy is urinating with minimal discomfort. She groans a little prior to urinating, but refuses any additional pain medication. She had to have her port flushed last week. She did moan a little and got teary eyed. It was good to see a reaction from her.

She has been lethargic lately and not resistant to procedures that she has fought in the past. I have had to administer enemas regularly to keep her bowels moving. It has always been a challenge in the past to do these. She wiggled, squirmed, and fought. For the past couple months, Emmy has given no reaction at all to the administering of the enemas. She lays quiet and still. Yesterday was the first time in a while she reacted to the enema. Although I don't want to see her uncomfortable, I was encouraged by her reaction.

Other than the urinary discomfort, Emmy is in no pain. She is comfortable. Her sleeping schedule is unpredictable. She is often up several times through the night.

Emmy is very frail. She has started to again have some issues with vomiting from time to time. She is down to forty pounds. Emmy is very tall for a four-year-old. She needs a size 6x/7 for length in her pants, but the waist is way too big. She needs more like a size 4/5 to fit her tummy area. When she was at her heaviest it was the exact opposite. She required a larger size to fit around her tummy and the legs would be way too long. She does not appear emaciated to look at her, just very, very thin. Her arms and legs are tiny, but she still has a round face with a little fullness in her cheeks.

102

I really notice how thin she is when I bathe and dress her. Emmy's back and bottom are all skin and bones. Her spine and ribs are visible through her skin. You can count each rib and vertebrae. Her bottom is so tiny and her hips bones are more prominent than her buttocks. Even with all these changes in her appearance, she is still the most beautiful little girl I have ever seen.

Emmy stares off into the distance, not focusing on anything. I feel like she is looking right through me. I am constantly asking her if she sees me and she always responds with her "Yes," but I can't help but wonder if she really sees me or just hears my voice. At these times, I often wonder if she sees angels. I have asked her this question in the past and she always responded "No." She has always told me she doesn't want to see angels. I think it was her way of telling me she was afraid.

She is staring off into the distance again today so I ask her if she sees angels. She tells me no. I then ask if she wants to see angels. She says "Yes." This is the first time ever she has said yes. I ask her if the angels come to see her, would she want to go play with them. She again says "Yes." Her answer gives me some sense of peace. I have been so worried she would be afraid when it was her time and the angels came. I pray her answer today indicates the opposite.

December 3, 2012

Today is a bit of a rough day for Emmy. She wakes with a spiked temperature. I have been medicating and using cold compresses to reduce her fever. It is been a quiet peaceful day with just the two of us. We spend the day snuggling in bed together, reading books, and listening to Christmas music. She is resting comfortably. Lying next to her seems to be the only way she will rest. She sleeps in small increments throughout the day and night. She usually wakes each evening around ten-thirty or eleven for a feeding. She will go back to sleep for a short period and then she is back up. She needs to have me next to her in her bed in order for her to feel safe. This doesn't allow for a lot sleep for either of us. We are working through it. We take naps together during the day when the boys are at school and Denny is at work. This is our Mommy and Emmy time.

Emmy has started vomiting again. She gets sick usually one time per day. I can only assume this is due to the cranial pressure from her tumor since nothing has changed with her diet. I pray the vomiting stops. She needs this nutrition for her already frail body. It hurts me to see her sick and know there is nothing I can do other than hold her to make it better. I look at Emmy sleeping and I am so thankful for every day with her. I know each day is a gift.

As her disease continues to progress, I am trying to prepare myself for the possibility of losing her. I am having a difficult time visualizing my life without her. Quite honestly, thinking about it causes me extreme anxiety. The walls feel like they are closing in on me, and I can't stop the tears from falling. I pace the floor trying to shake the thought of losing her from my mind. My heart hurts and I gasp for air. I feel like I can't breathe, can't catch my breath. I pray this isn't how it will feel for Emmy when she takes her last breath. It hurts so much.

I spend my days caring for Emmy the best I can. I try to stay busy, submerge myself in activities that keep me from thinking about what is to come. I try to focus on the positives. I try to make Emmy's time with us as special as possible. The quiet times are the hardest. My mind wanders to all of the possibilities, changes, symptoms, outcomes, and frankly, it terrifies me.

I will continue to do my best to stay strong, to create special memories daily, to find the beauty in the simplest of things, but most importantly to cherish time with my beautiful baby girl.

I will continue to pray Emmy remains comfortable throughout her journey. I will cherish the gift of "time" God has given to us. I am so thankful for every day and the blessings God has given me. May He bless you also.

God Bless you and Emmy. She has been such a fighter. I imagine this transition is going to be very scary for her. She wants to stay. This breaks my heart. My heart is heavy. I can't detach myself from Emmy. I've never met her, yet I feel connected to her so much. I love her with all of my heart and soul. I touch her pictures on my screen and pray. I sob for Emmy every day. My eyes ache.

Emmy has a presence about her. Something keeps telling me that I need to meet her, touch her hand, or hold her in my arms. It's almost as if God has already touched her and blessed her. I wanted there to be a Christmas Miracle for Emmy, but maybe Emmy is the Christmas Miracle. God is bringing us all to our knees, bringing us to him with prayers for Emmy, bringing some of us back to God and closer to Him.

December 7, 2012

Things seemed a little different today. Emmy doesn't want to eat much in the morning and she just looks different to me. I have a doctor's appointment for which I need to leave Emmy, so her Nana stays with her until I get home. It is hard to leave her. I am so afraid every time I have to leave or every time I fall asleep that it might be the last time I see Emmy awake. The last time she would respond to my questions. The last time I would see her beautiful big brown eyes. The last time I would see the rise and fall of her little chest. I need to be with Emmy when God chooses to take her home. I don't want her to be afraid. I pray God wouldn't choose to take her while I am gone. I can think of only Emmy until I return home.

When I get home, Emmy looks exhausted. Her breathing is a bit labored and she has a slight rattle.

"Has she been like this the whole time I was gone?" I ask my mom.

"Pretty much," Mom replies.

Emmy greets me as she always does, indicating she wants something to eat. I try giving her small amounts but she still ends up vomiting. She is unable to keep anything down. She doesn't want to eat anymore. She just stares at me. I feel as if she is trying to remember my face, as if it is the last time she would see me.

"Emmy, do you want Mommy to rock you in the rocking chair for a while?" Her eyes get huge with excitement. She moves them up and down continuously and vigorously as if to indicate "Yes, Yes, Yes!" I cradle Emmy in my arms just as I did so many years ago. We rock back and forth as I sing her favorite lullabies to her. Time passes so quickly. An hour flies by in what seems like a minute. I want to hold her in my arms with us staring at each other forever, but her exhaustion finally takes over and she wants to go back to her bed to sleep.

Denny comes into the room while I am rocking Emmy. I know he had planned to go hunting the next morning since it is the last day of buck season. "What time are you leaving in the morning and how long do you think you will be?" I ask.

"I don't know. Why?" he asks. His voice shakes a little as if he is worried what my answer might be.

I reply, "I don't know, but something seems different with Emmy. I can't really tell you what it is, but I don't think she is going to be with us much longer. I know you want to be here with her when God calls her home. I am just telling you what my gut feeling is in case you might want to stay home tomorrow."

He decides to wait until morning to see how Emmy is doing before he makes a decision.

I put Emmy in her jammies and place her in bed while I lay next to her. Since she is sleeping, I want to post a quick update on Facebook asking for continued prayers for Emmy. By the time I climb out of her bed and walk across the room, Emmy is awake again. She can't seem to settle, or let her body rest. She is only comfortable with me beside her in her bed, so this is where I stay.

She wakes and moans at me every time I move in the bed. She is so afraid I am going to go sleep on the couch instead of beside her. I promise her I will sleep beside her all night. At three a.m. I get out of her bed to use the restroom. She again wakes and moans at me. I assure her I will be right back. I climb back in to Emmy's bed and cradle her in my arms. She falls back asleep within seconds. This is how we sleep into the morning.

I wake around eight a.m. when Jesse comes downstairs. Emmy is in a deep sleep. She doesn't seem to move when I crawl out of her bed. She doesn't seem to respond to Jesse's noises while he plays next to her bedside. I wonder if she is sleeping so deeply because her little body is just so exhausted or has she slipped into an unresponsive state. I try to wake Emmy with no response. At this time I wonder if our three a.m. interaction might have been the last. I post the update to Facebook asking for continued prayers and comfort for the next part of Emmy's journey.

December 7, 2012

Lillian Sanden Glass

Dear Lord, please hear our prayers as we lift up our voices to pray for our little angel Emmy Mott and for her family.

Dear Lord, if it be Your will, please grant more precious moments for this family so that Emmy can celebrate Jesse's birthday and be with her family for the celebration of your Son's birth this Christmas

Dear Lord, this child has touched our hearts and brought us all together in prayer. Lord, we have seen so many miracles in this journey with Emmy; she has inspired so many of us with her gentle grace, her courage, and her love for her family and their love for her. We are so thankful for the gift of Emmy and the chance to witness Your Greatness in the face of this precious child, she radiates with Your Love. *She leads us all to You, Lord.* This small child has brought us to our knees in both prayer for healing and in praise for all the blessings You have granted. Thank You, Lord, for all the mercies You have shown us, please hear our prayers. In Jesus's name we pray. Amen.

To my granddaughter "Emily Mott"
By Bruce Brodowski

Oh precious child
Your legacy
You've touched the hearts
Of those who see

Your beacon of light
Your beautiful smile
Of such delight
Just for a while

My heart cries out
With one word "Why"
So little time
Before good bye

Will you dance with angels?
In a glorious place
Will you hear choirs singing?
Will you kiss Jesus's face?

Soon happiness and love
Will be your reward
In heavens above
All in one accord

Sleep now sweet princess
Tomorrow fear not
Your peace is coming
Precious Emily Mott

December 8, 2012

I fear Emmy has slipped into a coma. This morning Emmy did not wake. She is currently unresponsive and resting peacefully. Her body feels like she is on fire. The ear thermometer reads 105.8 degrees, but her beautiful little feet are like ice cubes. I immediately start medicating Emmy, alternating between Tylenol® and Motrin® to try to bring down her temperature. I strip her down to a T-shirt, undies and a light sheet. I apply cold compresses to her forehead, the nape of her neck, armpits and chest area.

I decide to give Hospice a call to let them know what is happening. I explain all her symptoms and what I have been doing to treat them. I tell them I didn't need a visit, but want them to be aware that it appears as though Emmy is now in an unresponsive state.

Emmy's breathing changes. She has labored breathing. It seems slower and longer in between breaths. She is not responding to our voices or touch, but I know she hears me. She looks like a peaceful sleeping angel.

I will be praying this part of the journey is peaceful and comfortable for Emmy. I pray she is not afraid. I pray she knows it is okay to go. I pray she knows we will all be okay. I pray she knows it won't be long until we are all together again. I pray she knows how much we all love her. I pray I told her it enough to get her through until we see each other again. I pray she knows it isn't good-bye; it is "I love you and I'll miss you, but I will see you later."

Every once in a while she would make a little noise. I have been administering additional medications to keep her comfortable. I decide to give her additional pain medications and meds to make her less anxious. I want to be sure she is comfortable since she is no longer able to indicate to me any pain she is feeling. I stay with Emmy every minute I can at her side. I receive a phone call asking permission for a prayer vigil to occur at our home in the evening. I welcome the thoughts and prayers for Emmy and our family.

*****

The Vigil

Lillian Sanden Glass

Ever since I was directed to Emmy's Facebook page, I have been in love with Emmy Mott. I started following Emmy's Journey in March. NEVER has a story about anything or anyone that I personally did not know affected me the way Emmy and her mom Tammy have. I know that God drew me to this page and then to Tammy. God wanted me to know Emmy and all throughout this I still had never met them, I didn't want to intrude, didn't want to break down in front of Emmy, I just didn't know what to do.

When I read the post about Emmy, God again spoke to me to go to her. I decided to not bother Tammy at this time so I looked at her friends on her page and God led me to Kim Morrow. I sent her a friend request and a message that I felt the need to hold a prayer vigil for Emmy. She wrote back that she also felt the same need, she called someone else, and that person had the same thought. God brought us together.

It was amazing to the point that I was crying and shaking at the same time that God led me to just the person I needed with one try. In a few minutes time Kim had set a prayer service up for six-thirty p.m. We got busy calling and spreading the word to be at the Mott home. I am so thankful for how quickly we were able to pull this together. It was through God that this happened; he was leading all of us.

*****

Jennifer King

In the quiet of the bitterly cold night, fifteen people, or maybe more, stood right outside where Emmy was laying. We all braved through it. Some people had brought paper bags and candles for the vigil and lined part of the driveway with their lit candles. The wind blew some candles out while others stayed lit. There were pretty icicle lights on the house that looked like they were dripping.

My daughter Emily had brought a sock monkey to give to Emmy. I knew Emmy probably would never get to see it but I let my daughter Emily give it to her anyways. It meant so much to my child to give and care for another. Before we started praying, my daughter gave Emmy the monkey.

As we prayed, a lot of us felt as if Emmy was our child as well. We were fighting back tears while knowing that Emmy would be leaving soon and so, so young. Not understanding God's reasons, but loving and caring about her anyways. We prayed for the family because the grieving process is going to take awhile. The anger that they may feel at some point. The ability we have to lift them up in our prayers and supporting them as we can.

Jesse and JP were by Emmy's bedside. Seeing Jesse through the window wanting to share his cheese balls with all of us put a smile on all of our faces. People had talked about how JP and Jesse wouldn't understand all of this and how Denny and Tammy would have to maybe keep telling JP where Emmy was and how that would cause them pain to have to say that again and again.

I hold the sights of Emmy's parents by Emmy's bedside last night in my heart for the rest of my days. I think I knew something was happening while we were praying. We could see through the window in Denny's face the expressions of nervousness and wanting to hurry to Emmy's side. Denny rushed over to her with a wet red towel. He may have been wiping Emmy's face to help with the fever a bit.

Everyone there last night prayed for healing for the family. Many talked about what if it was your child. None of us could imagine what Denny and Tammy have gone through. I can't. We sang "Silent Night" and "Jesus Loves Me." It felt very fitting.

There was a man that came to pray with us and Helping Hands. I think he was a pastor. He had trouble holding back the tears as well.

A couple went into the house just after we had finished singing. They went to Emmy's bedside, held her hand, and kissed her good-bye.

The vigil ended at seven-thirty p.m. Denny came out to thank all of us for our support throughout all of this. Tammy at the end said thank you out the door but was sad and quiet.

*****

Lillian Sanden Glass

I don't know how many were there in the dark, between fifteen and twenty, I would say. A pastor from the Baptist church was there. I was so emotional I don't remember his name.

It was a chilly night and it had been raining off and on all day. However, when we all got to the Mott's house, there was no more rain and luminaries were lit. I met people that I have commented with on Emmy and Tammy's Facebook pages, people I met for the first time last night. We could see the family inside with Emmy. Denny Mott came out and thanked us for being there and how much they appreciated it. Jesse opened the door to come out for a few seconds and then he watched us through the window. This must be so confusing for Jesse, he is just turning three and Emmy is not just a big sister, she is his best friend. My heart hurts for him and what he is losing.

The pastor spoke about Emmy and her journey to heaven and we recited the 23rd Psalm. He then prayed and then some of us prayed and spoke of memories with Emmy. We then sang "Silent Night." I hope it helped those that were there, it was so hard to accept and admit that this was maybe Emmy's last time here.

Tammy graciously offered that anyone that wanted to go in to see Emmy could go in. So, for the first time, I was meeting this precious child and her parents. I have felt like I knew them from all of Tammy's posts and pictures throughout this journey, but it doesn't prepare you. Emmy looked beautiful but so tiny and frail in her bed. I was able to hold her hand and tell her that I loved her. I was able to say in person to her parents how much I loved their daughter and what a profound effect she has been in my life. It was a very emotional time for me. I thank the Lord for pushing me, leading me, and speaking to me.

*****

Diania Kjar Janoski

Saturday night I had the honor of attending a prayer vigil for Emmy Mott. I didn't know what to expect but I just knew I had to be there. I hadn't yet met Emmy or her family, but I was one of the many, many people that prayed heavily for her.

I can't explain my drawness to this child. I can't explain my feelings for her that have become so overpowering for me. Maybe it's because I have four daughters of my own, maybe it's because she is a child, maybe because my own soul needed something. I don't know but, for whatever reason, I am forever grateful.

I am also forever grateful for Tammy and Denny allowing me to come into their home and allowing me to meet Emmy. I gave her a kiss, told her I loved her and I held her tiny warm hand.

It was very cold out and the wind had picked up. Some of us couldn't feel our hands as we held our candles and flashlights. But it didn't matter. We had to give our pleas to God the Father one more time.

As we were listening to the pastor, I watched Tammy thru the window tending to Emmy's needs. I saw Denny walking around, nervous. I saw little Jesse looking at us thru the window, wanting to offer cheese puffs. He looks like Emmy. I kept wondering what was going thru his little mind.

I couldn't stop crying. I looked at the cool lights Tammy had on the house. Christmas lights that mimicked icicles. My eyes were so full of water that they looked huge to me.

114

I am grateful for the new friends I have made thru Emmy. Unbelievable.

If I have learned anything from God THRU Emmy, it's that my heart has not become cold from cancer and death. I have lost so many of my family to cancer and I had found myself becoming hard. Emmy taught me I still have a heart and I still care, very much.

Thank you, Angel Emmy, and thank you, Motts, for allowing me and so many others to be a part of this journey. And, as much as it hurts and as much as myself and others have wept and cried out to God, I am thankful for Emmy. Her life and death were not in vain. Thank you, Emmy Girl. I pray you knew and know how very, very special you are and what you did to so many of us. I love you.

*****

Tammy

We decide to call family and friends to let them know what is happening in case they want to come see Emmy. Many visitors come to our home throughout the day. The last of our family leaves around six p.m.. This is the time we start having guests arrive for the prayer vigil. People light luminaries for the vigil. The driveway in front of our home glows in the darkness from all the lit candles. The pastor comes in to meet our family before the vigil starts and prays with us. I sit beside Emmy in her bed as I continue to watch her breathing become more and more shallow. JP and Jesse curiously watch the people through the window. I think I hear "Silent Night" being sung outside. It echoes in the distance while I whisper in Emmy's ear, "I love you so much, sweet baby girl. It is okay for you to go. Mommy, Daddy, JP and Jesse will be right behind you. You don't have to be afraid. The angels will take care of you. They will guide you to heaven and before you can turn around, we will all be together. You are going to love it there. You won't feel sick anymore. You will be able to run, laugh, sing, and dance again. You will be able to play with lots of new friends and animals. If you can imagine how much fun we had when we went to Sea World, this will be so much better than that. We all love you so much and will be with you always."

I keep whispering repeatedly in Emmy's ear how much I love her as I lay beside her, cradling her and caressing her cheek.

All her body parts that are rigid due to the tumor are now relaxed and move with ease when I manipulate them. I keep watching for the rise and fall of Emmy's chest to assure she is breathing. Her head is back and mouth wide open. It seems strange to see her mouth open since her jaws have been clenched for so long. Her lips quiver with each breath. Emmy's breaths grow shorter and shorter with increasing time passing between each one. She is so relaxed and looks so peaceful. I feel it won't be long before God takes her home.

The vigil ends and a few people come inside to see Emmy. Everyone is gone by seven-thirty p.m. At seven forty-five I lay beside Emmy with her dad and brothers at her side as she takes her last breath. I have read so many stories of what the last hours, minutes, seconds are like for other children who have passed before Emmy. I wanted to prepare myself for what could happen. Emmy's passing is so peaceful. There is no struggle, no pain, and no fear. I thank God for making the last of her time here on the Earth so comfortable for her. I can't help but think about how close Emmy's passing is to the end of the prayer vigil, just fifteen minutes between the two. It is as if they all prayed her Home.

*****

Lillian Sanden Glass

I left at seven-thirty p.m. Emmy went to the Lord and her Heavenly Home at seven forty-five p.m. I still can't get over that. God led us there!!!! God was in that room with us, we were in the presence of Our Father and this Precious Child who was receiving her Wings. Fly, Precious Emmy, Fly High, sing and laugh with the Angels. Feel the Love and Peace as The Lord holds you in His Arms. We Love You, Baby Girl.

116

Tammy

We make all the necessary calls to family members. Family members come back to the house to see Emmy one last time before the funeral home takes her away. I wait for about an hour before I call Hospice. We all want some more time with Emmy. I know once I make the call to Hospice, it will start the process for her to go. I don't want to leave her side. I keep hugging her and kissing her.

Hospice arrives and we start the necessary paperwork. They ask if I am ready for them to call the funeral home. Am I ready? How can I ever be ready? I tell them yes and return to Emmy.

By ten-thirty p.m. Van Matre Funeral Home pulls into our driveway. Bill and Billy Van Matre come into our home to talk with us and to see Emmy. They give us as much time as we need with Emmy. They answer questions and then ask if we are ready for them to take her. We tell them yes. Denny wants to carry Emmy out to the hearse. He wraps her in a white furry blanket and carries her to the gurney on our front porch. She is strapped in and taken to the hearse. Denny, Jesse and I watch from the front porch as they place her lifeless body into the back of the hearse and drive down the road. We watch until we can't see its lights anymore.

All is quiet and still. We start to return into the house when Jesse runs back out yelling, "Emmy, Emmy, Emmy!" Jesse sat on the front porch calling her name, "Emmy, Emmy, Emmy." His cries break the silence in the night. It tore my heart apart. I can't help but start crying too. I told him, "The angels have taken Emmy to be with Jesus now. We will miss her, but she will always be in our hearts. " I hold him on my lap as we swing back and forth on the porch swing. I run my fingers through his hair as he lays his head on my chest.

Jesse said, "Emmy gone."

I say, "I know, buddy. Mommy misses Sissy too. She is in heaven now with Jesus. We will all be together again one day. When we are missing Emmy we can share stories, look at photos, or watch videos. Emmy will be with us always. At night when we close our eyes we can think about Emmy and maybe she will visit us in our dreams."

He continued calling for her and looking for her throughout the house. I followed him and found him looking for her in JP's room. I scooped him up and held him so tight. I couldn't stop crying. He kept saying, "Emmy gone, Emmy gone."

I said, "I know, baby. It is hard, but Emmy no longer has any boo boos. She is with Jesus now. He will keep her safe until we can all be together again."

Jesse walked over to JP's bookshelf and picked up a white crucifix. He told me, "Emmy gone, Jesus," and he pointed to Jesus on the cross. He then climbed into the middle of my bed. He drifted off to sleep clenching the crucifix in his hand while I ran my fingers through his hair. I pray that night Emmy will visit Jesse. He is already missing her so much and needs comforting by his big Sissy. This is going to be harder for him than I ever anticipated. I thought he was too young to really understand, but I guess I was wrong.

I know things are going to be chaotic for the next few weeks. Family will be coming from out of town. We need to get everything ready for the funeral. After the funeral we will be busy finishing getting ready for Christmas. At some point things are going to settle down and get quiet again. The boys would have time to realize Emmy is gone. I know they will have questions and wonder where she is. I know it will be hard for all of us for awhile. We are going to have to figure out how to start again, how to create a new "normal" for our family. It won't be easy for any of us, but I know with God and our angel Emmy at our side we can get through anything.

*****

Cheryl Beuchat

Cheryl shared this poem with us – it's one that's been circulating the Internet for many years for bereavement, and has not been credited with an author that we were able to find.

Mommy, please don't look so sad,
Daddy, please don't cry.
Cause I'm in the arms of Jesus,
And he sings me lullabies.

Please try not to question God,
Don't think he is unkind.
Don't think he sent me to you
and then changed his mind.

You see I'm a special child,
Am needed up above.
I'm the special gift you gave Him,
a product of your love.

I'll always be there with you,
So watch the sky at night.
Look for the brightest star
And know that's my halo's brilliant light.

You'll see me in the morning frost
That mists your window pane.
That's me in the summer showers,
I'll be dancing in the rain.

When you feel a gentle breeze
from a gentle wind that blows
Know that it's me
Planting a kiss upon your nose.

When you see a child playing
And your heart feels a tug,
Don't be sad, Mommy,
That's just me giving your heart a hug.

So Mommy, don't look so sad
And Daddy, please don't cry.
I'm in the arms of Jesus
And he sings me lullabies.
   -Author Unknown

December 9, 2012

We finalize plans at the funeral home. We are all adjusting to the change in our lives. JP doesn't understand much of what has happened. He hasn't asked about Emmy. We told him last night that Emmy has gone to be with Jesus. Maybe he just accepts this without question. Jesse, on the other hand, is having a harder time than I expected. He doesn't understand where his sissy is.

Denny is holding it together. He is so strong. He is my rock. He is there to comfort me when I am feeling overwhelmed. I know his time to grieve will come and I will be there for him just as he has been there for me.

It has been hard to know what to do with myself today. I am missing Emmy like crazy. I cried so hard this morning. I couldn't breathe, couldn't catch my breath. My heart hurt with a pain like nothing I have ever felt before. I paced the living room trying to think of something that would make me stop, but I couldn't. All I could think about was how much I missed my baby girl. I had to pull it together for the boys. I want them to know it is okay to be sad and okay to cry, but I didn't want to scare them. I had a good cry, more like an uncontrollable sob.

I then thought of how happy Emmy must be now. Free, free of all pain, free to run, play, sing, dance, and eat lots and lots of ice cream. She will turn around and, in a blink of an eye, we will be with her again. I know friends and family who passed before her were waiting with open arms. I know she is experiencing a love like never before. I will take comfort in this.

You have your wings now, baby girl. You are free. Fly, fly, fly. "I love you and I'll miss you, but *I will see you later.*"

*****

December 10, 2012

Steve Kenyon

Following Emmy's journey and hearing about honest courage and genuine heartbreak over their loss, I cannot help but feel like it is my loss as well. I never knew this little girl or her family, but I feel connected somehow to all of them and I wish with every wish I could make that this would all just go away and bring our little friend back. God has a plan in all of this and we try to understand, but it just ... well ... it just sucks.

I have learned throughout this entire ordeal that my heart is not hardened by the abusers and my love for mankind is still intact. I wish I could say thank you to young Emmy for showing me that it is okay to cry and it is okay to be sad, but beyond all of that, I am forever thankful for the family's courage to share their story with us. This young girl had more love and friendship in her four short years than a lot of adults have in an entire lifetime.

Thank you, Father God, for this precious little girl you allowed us to know. Thank you, God, for reminding all of us how important it is to love each other. Later today, I am going to have a bowl of ice cream in memory of this little girl and I will pray for the family for the days and weeks and months and beyond that, You dear God, will give them your peace and comfort.

*****

We stare out the window through our tears as the thought hits us … She is gone, the battle is over, the house feels empty, our hearts are broken. We try to be brave for the little ones, but they seem to know something is wrong. All we can do is fight back the tears in front of them and try as we may, the tears still fall …

While we are watching the rain pelt the window and hear the wind howling outside, we catch a glimpse, ever so brief, of a rainbow. While we say good-bye through our grief, we can, if we listen hard enough and quiet our hearts, hear the angel's voices in a quiet hush turn toward the gates of heaven and just as we say to ourselves she is gone, the angel's faces light up and in a chorus of song and laughter cry out, "Here she comes … she is home!" And with that she stepped into heaven, and she kissed the face of God.

I am saddened to hear of Emily's passing. She fought a valiant fight and gave it all she had … I don't know if this helps, but the way I think about it is she did not lose the battle, she won the battle. She stepped through the gates this morning and heard the words we all long to hear one day … "Well done, good and faithful servant … enter into the joy of your lord."

December 11, 2012

It is two-thirty in the morning. The house is so quiet and still. I can't stop thinking about you, baby girl. Daddy and I have been spending our time planning your funeral. We have so many photos and personal items of yours to share with people at the funeral home to celebrate the miracle that is you. Things have been so crazy these past couple of days. There hasn't been a lot of time to just sit and think. Friday and Saturday are going to be so hard for all of us, but I know you will be looking down on us, smiling, holding our hands, helping us through.

Max is sleeping in his favorite spot, under the Christmas tree. He may love Christmas almost as much as you. We took the hospital bed down yesterday. It was so hard for Jesse to see it and not ask where you were. Even though it was all taken apart and sitting in the living room with the mattress on its side, Max still found a way to finagle a way on top to sleep. He has been looking for you. He misses his sleeping buddy.

Jesse asked about you again this morning. I told him you were resting in the arms of Jesus now. We were lying in bed trying to settle to sleep. That is when his little mind started to wander. He kept asking for you again. Daddy and I again told him you were in heaven with Jesus. I told him you were running, and jumping, and playing, and singing, and dancing. I told him if he closed his eyes, he would be able to see you and talk with you in his dreams. I told him you were with us always. He said he misses you and he drifted off to sleep snuggling with Daddy. I hope you visit him tonight. I know he would love to see you.

JP doesn't say much. He watched me as I started sorting through some of your things. I wondered what he was thinking. Mommy has talked with you about JP before. You know JP is special and it is hard for him to say the things he feels. Please know that even though he doesn't ask as Jesse does, he still loves you so much and misses you like crazy.

The snow is softly falling outside my window. It makes me think of you and how much you loved the snow. It made me think of a winter song we would listen to. I am playing it for you now. I hope you enjoy listening to it again.

It is really getting late now. I am going to try to get some rest. As I drift to sleep, I will be thinking of your beautiful face. I will be looking for you in my dreams. Good night, my love. I love you and I miss you, but I will see you later.

December 11, 2012

Bruce

I sit here this morning feeling so very guilty that I am not spending the time with God that I promised I would. I have not been perseverant in my prayer time. Getting all caught up in the world around me and the needs of my family. Words bounce around in my head like ping pong balls trying to come together into sentences of a …a paragraph or poem. The overwhelming desire to write, to create, to place down on the paper my thoughts. Maybe that is God? Maybe we are spending time together. Maybe He is communicating to me this morning.

A church friend of ours has told us that she had a dream of Jesus pushing Emmy on a swing in a playground full of children. Running, laughing, playing with overwhelming Joy. I have had people tell me from their vision experiences that the living water in heaven dances and wraps around you lovingly like a blanket. The colors of the flowers are every color you can imagine and even more. As they sway in the wind, they make sounds that come together to make heavenly music. Music like no other that we have heard before. What do you suppose Emmy's mansion looks like? A castle like the one at Disneyworld? One can only wonder.

We get so busy being busy. We make important the unimportant, allowing the things of this world to become overwhelming. We neglect to take time to listen. To listen to the deep still quiet voice inside us that is whispering ever so softly, "I love you, You are my precious child in whom I am well pleased." Yes, today, let me sit in the swing that Jesus is pushing. Swinging higher to the sky. Fly away, fly away, Fly, fly, fly.

Emmy touched the hearts of thousands of people all over the world.

December 16, 2012
Emmy's Facebook Page Statistics

Total Likes	2,970
Friends of Fans	805,322
People Talking About This	2,694
Weekly Total Reach	72,230

Countries

67,370	United States of America
2,018	Australia
808	Canada
482	United Kingdom
146	Germany
74	Philippines
71	El Salvador
69	South Africa
66	New Zealand
44	Indonesia
43	Italy
41	India
39	Japan
38	Mexico
37	France
35	Ireland
32	Spain
31	Portugal
31	Brazil
26	Sweden

Languages

68,722	English (US)
2,622	English (UK)
163	Spanish
91	German
55	Spanish (Spain)
52	French (France)
30	English (Pirate)
30	Italian
27	Portuguese (Brazil)
26	Portuguese (Portugal)
25	Dutch
24	Indonesian
17	Polish
16	Swedish
15	Danish
12	Norwegian (Bokmal)
11	Turkish
11	Greek
11	Japanese
8	Russian

I will see you later

December 16, 2012

We all got up this morning and visited Emmy at the cemetery. I feel closer to her there. We put a flower arrangement from her funeral at her gravesite. Other flowers were placed on the graves of some family members. We placed a small arrangement on the grave of Emmy's namesake, her great, great grandmother Emily Mott. While walking back toward the car, Denny noticed a memorial stone for a five-year-old little girl. I felt a need to share flowers with her too. I pulled a white rose, pink lily and blue butterfly from Emmy's arrangement and placed them at this little girl's grave. I can see Emmy in heaven with this little girl playing and dancing. I am sure she is introducing her as her new best friend. Every time she would meet a new little friend she would always tell me, "Mommy, she is my new best friend," even if she hardly knew them. She was definitely a social butterfly.

Things are beginning to settle down, and I am missing Emmy a lot. I find myself almost forgetting she is not here. I folded clothes today. When I put them into the clothesbasket I instinctively saved the spot in the basket where I always placed hers, only to realize there was none. I saw a commercial with a little girl who lost her front tooth and all I could think was Emmy never lost any teeth. She never got to experience the Tooth Fairy. My heart began to hurt with the pain of missing her. Christmas is going to be hard for all of us, but we need to make it a joyful time. This was Emmy's absolute favorite time of year, and I know she will be with us in spirit.

I know that as time goes on, the hurt and the pain of her passing will decrease, but the longing to have her with me again will never subside.

My Emmy girl, until we meet again. I love you and I'll miss you, but *I will see you later.*

December 18, 2012

Hello, my sweet Emmy. Daddy and I visited you at the cemetery again today. Did you see us? Mommy has been there every morning. When we came today the most beautiful big white snowflakes were falling from the sky. It made me smile to think about how much you loved the snow. I am so glad we got to make snow angels together.

I keep feeling a need to come to you there. It is still where I feel closest to you. Once Mommy goes back to work, I won't be able to come see you every day. Please know that even if I am not there, I am thinking of you always. I love you so much.

Yesterday we celebrated Jesse's birthday. It was a fire truck theme. We all know how much Jesse loves fire trucks. We all missed you. Things just didn't feel the same without you here. I know how much you loved birthday parties with cake and especially the ice cream, your favorite. Jesse ate extra for you. I know he is missing you so much. He asked about you on the way home from school today. I told him you are in heaven with Jesus dancing with the angels, but it is hard for him to understand. He wants his "best buddy" back to play with him.

After Jesse's party we went to see the Rieger Christmas light show in Girard. It was amazing. The show lasted about a half hour. So many bright lights synchronized to the beat of the music. It was awesome. I wish we had the chance to take you there. We shouldn't have tried to wait to go until Jesse's birthday for the firework show. We should have taken you as soon as we found out about it. You would have had a chance to enjoy it too. I know you would have loved it.

Good-bye for now, Emmy girl. I love you and I'll miss you, but *I will see you later.*

December 20, 2012

Oh my goodness Em, it was so windy at the cemetery today. Mommy had to pick up your flowers and Christmas wreath because they blew over. I am sure the wind will blow the flowers over again by tomorrow when I come for my visit. The wind is so strong tonight. The rain started and the snow is coming.

Jesse sure was missing you today. He asked for you at bedtime last night and called for you several times on the way to daycare. I again told him you were in heaven with Jesus. He kept telling me "No, no." I said, "I know buddy, Mommy misses her bunches, too." He looked so sad. I don't know what else to do except to keep telling him where you are and reassuring him we will see you again someday. JP is missing you too. He doesn't say much, but he keeps taking out your photo albums and looking through them. I guess he feels closer to you when he sees you.

Jesse had his Christmas party at daycare today. We took in cookies, class treats, and presents. I know how much you loved your school Christmas party. We gave the school a butterfly kit for Christmas. They will be able to hatch them in the spring when it is warmer. When they release the butterflies, maybe the butterflies will choose to live in your butterfly garden. Whenever your friends see a butterfly, they will always be able to think of you.

Mommy and Daddy did some last minute shopping today. Nana watched your brothers. We saw a movie at the theater and went to dinner. It was the first time in a very long time Mommy and Daddy have done anything without children. It was hard not to think about you. Our conversation still seemed to revolve around you, JP and Jesse. I can't help thinking in the back of my mind that I am constantly forgetting to do something. I am lost without you here. When we were in the store I kept gravitating to the girl's clothing. I have no idea why. I go there without even thinking. I start looking through clothes for things that I know you would like then I realize you are no longer here for me to buy them for you. Mommy always loved shopping for you, especially shoes. I know how much you loved your shoes. The brighter and more sparkly, the better. You had more shoes in your closet than most adult women. I miss shopping with my best girl. It was our special time together. Nana liked coming too. You always had a way of convincing one of us to buy you something before we left the store.

It is going to be a hard Christmas without you this year. Our lives will never be the same. I will always miss you and be thinking of you, but as time goes by I think I'll miss you most at Christmas time. We will all be thinking of you. I hope to see you in my dreams. I love you and I'll miss you, but *I will see you later.*

December 22, 2012

Mommy, Daddy, and the boys came to see you at the cemetery this morning. We had to walk back because the snow was so deep. The backhoe had just dug another fresh gravesite. It appeared as though another funeral would be taking place today. It makes Mommy sad to think of another family without a loved one so close to Christmas. Whoever it is, I know you will welcome them and our cousin Viola who arrived at heaven's doors yesterday morning. She too will be missed by so many.

Mommy cleared the snow off your wreath and flowers. I can't believe the flowers still look so nice, even with the cold and snow. They have been sitting at your gravesite for a week now. The pink rose in your arrangement looked so bright against the fresh white snow.

Lois at Treasured Memories put together a special pink rose for me to bring to you. She took extra special care to wrap it so it would withstand the weather. She is so thoughtful. I think it looks beautiful. I put it right next to your name marker.

JP wanted to do something special for you. He made a snow angel for you right next to your gravesite. I took a picture, but it was a little hard to see the outline. We are going to make reindeer food today so Santa can find our house on Christmas Eve. I know how much you loved making the reindeer food and sprinkling it on the snow. It looks like the snow is going to stop for a little while. Mommy will try to bring you some reindeer food and a little Christmas tree.

I can't believe it has been two weeks now since you received your angel wings. It is strange to me to think about how time can go by so fast and so slow at the same time. The past two weeks feel like a blur. Everything happened so quickly. At the same time, it feels like an eternity since I have seen your beautiful big brown eyes and rosy cheeks or heard you laugh.

We are all missing you like crazy, but I know, for you, we will be together before you can realize we were even apart. I love and I'll miss you, but *I will see you later.*

THE TITUSVILLE HERALD
Titusville, PA

Daughter's Short Life Gives Family Lessons and Miracles
By Tammy Mott

On April 27, 2008, God sent a miracle to this world. He blessed our lives by sending this angel to us, to care for until he called her home.

Her name was Emily "Emmy" Katherine Mott. She was the most beautiful little girl. She had the biggest dark brown eyes and the rosiest red cheeks. Her smile could melt my heart every time she looked at me. She was so full of life, energy, determination, independence and love. Raising her was not without its challenges, but well worth the rewards.

God sent us Emmy so she could teach us all. She touched so many lives, and was an inspiration to thousands of people all over the world. The lessons she taught were different for each of us.

For some, it was bringing them closer to God and spending more time in prayer. For others, it was finding the beauty in the simple things and not getting caught up in the hustle and bustle of everyday life. For some, it was appreciating the time we have with our loved ones; holding our children closer; saying "I love you" more; forgiving others; generosity; and living each day to the fullest. Emmy taught us so many beautiful life lessons. She has brought out the best in all of us.

We all spent so much time cherishing, loving and caring for Emmy. She brought our community closer together. She blessed all our lives. She is now our special angel.

We all watched over her, and now it is her time to watch over all of us. I take comfort in knowing she is with me always.

I know Emmy is with us every day. I see her in the brilliant colors of the rainbow; in the soft fluttering of a butterfly's wings; in the glistening of the bright white falling snow; and in her little brother Jesse's big brown eyes, rosy cheeks and infectious smile. He is the spitting image of his sissy.

I hear her in the melodic tune of her wind chimes as they gently blow in the wind; in the pitter-patter of little feet as they run though the house; in every Ho-ho-ho Santa shout; and in the laughter of her big brother, JP, as he and Jesse chase each other through the house.

I feel her in the tears that gently roll down my face when I think of her; in the warmth of the sunshine as it beams upon my cheek; in the hugs and kisses I receive from her brothers; and in the ache I feel in my heart from missing her so much. I can truly say I have loved someone so much it hurts.

Emmy is a special gift sent from God for all of us. I will cherish this gift always. She is my Christmas miracle. I have learned so much from her. I am a better person and mother for having had the privilege of loving and caring for this amazing little girl. I pray, as time passes, I will always honor Emmy by practicing the life lessons she has taught. I hope you will all do the same.

Hold your loved ones a little closer; our time with them is so precious, and sometimes shorter than we ever can imagine.

Merry Christmas, sweet baby girl. In the blink of an eye, we will all be together again. I love you, and I'll miss you, but *I will see you later.*

Tammy Mott, of Cambridge Springs, state, is the mother of Emmy Mott. Emmy was diagnosed with an inoperable brain stem tumor. She passed away on December 8, 2012. She was four years old.

Article originally appeared December 24, 2012 in The Titusville Herald. Used with permission from the publisher.

Fly Away, Fly Away, Fly, Fly, Fly

By Bruce Brodowski

I see the bright light
It's blinding me
Obscuring my sight
Of Emily

A choir of angels
Melodious singing
Starry sky twinkles
Church bells ringing

Children playing careless
Their laughter bring
Laughter to sweet Jesus
Pushing the swing

Oh, there she is
Swinging high to the sky
Fly away, fly away
Fly, fly, fly

Postscript

Bruce Brodowski

I am retired and now in full time healing prayer ministry. As a minister and missionary I was not prepared to come head to head with the sovereignty of God. I believe in a loving God. I teach about a loving God. I teach that through God's love healing occurs. I believe in God's word in Scriptures. I believe in Isaiah that the blind will see, the lame will walk, the deaf will hear, and the captives will be set free.

What I don't believe in is the theology of the suffering servant. I don't believe that we are made to suffer and lift our suffering up to Jesus to suffer for souls. What loving Father would create a son or daughter for the purpose of suffering?

I prayed over Emmy several times for healing. People all over the world that have successful healing ministries prayed for divine healing. Emmy still died, leaving us with this big hole in our soul and a huge question Why?

I watched for forty-one weeks what God was doing. Through it all, Emmy's smile and her eyes radiated unconditional love. God used her to touch thousands of hearts in many countries. People who had stopped prayer in their life or had left the church were suddenly on their knees in tears. Her big brown eyes melted the hardest of hearts. Her smile was the beacon of light of her joy.

I was humbled. I teach about God's love but here I was witnessing His love through a four year old child. She just happened to be my granddaughter. In forty-one weeks Emmy taught more by example than I could teach in a week-long seminar.

I pray that Emmy's story will change your life. May the Lord bless you and keep you. May the Lord make His face to shine upon you, and be gracious to you. May the Lord lift up His countenance upon you, and give you peace.

And Emmy girl, I will see you later.

*****

Tammy Brodowski Mott

Many times significant things happen to us that make us look at life differently. It is unfortunate it often takes something devastating for us to realize the things in our lives that are most important. My whole world changed. I look at things differently than I used to. I see the beauty in simple things now that I have overlooked before; the brilliant colors of the rainbow, the beauty of a butterfly, the crisp cool feel of a snowflake, the sound of the gentle wind blowing through the trees. I try to experience these things as if every time is the first time. I try not to take anything for granted anymore. I try to live each day as if it could be my last. I make sure to let my family know how much I love them. I try to appreciate the gifts I have been given. I try to remember that these gifts come from God and with Him all things are possible. He is my strength.

I hope that in sharing Emmy's story with you, it might inspire you to look at your life differently. Take nothing for granted and appreciate all your gifts and blessings. Take time to cherish the things in your lives that are most important. There is that word again, that special gift, *time*. We truly have so much for which to be thankful. May we all remember this daily. Give thanks and praise to Jesus for He deserves Glory, Honor, and Praise. May the legacy of Emmy be that her story will change your life.

Emmy Stories

Emmy and I were lying in bed reading a bedtime story. The book was *Heaven is For Real*. She loved the picture of Jesus's white rainbow horse.

"Mommy, me want a horse," she said.

"We can't get a horse, Emmy," I replied.

"Why?" she asked.

"I know you want a pet, but a horse isn't an animal you can keep in the house and snuggle. It is too big. We would need to have a barn to keep it in and we don't have one. Also, we can't afford a horse. They are very expensive to buy and to feed."

Emmy replies, "Mom, me have an idea. Just go to the bank. They give you money there."

*****

Emmy got a kitten as a present for her fourth birthday. After a month, he needed to go to the veterinarian for his first visit.

"Emmy, Max needs to go the doctors for a check-up," I said.

"Why?" she replies.

"Max is just a baby and he needs to go to the doctors for check-ups just like you needed to do when you were a baby. The doctor will check him over. Max will need to get a shot."

"Mommy, me will tell him if he is very brave he might get a sticker and a lollipop."

*****

Emmy has always had difficulty with her speech. This made it hard for her to sing songs. The only song she would sing was called "Big Poppa" by Biggie Smalls. It was comical to hear her sing it. I would sing the chorus, "*I love it when you call me Big Poppa*." She would echo me by singing out, "*Big Poppa, Big Poppa, Big Poppa.*" We would sing this often. One day I was singing the chorus as I always had before, "*I love it when you call me Big Poppa.*" Emmy chimed in singing, "*Big Poppa, Big Poppa Big Poppa.*" Then something clicked with Emmy. I sang the chorus again, "*I love it when you call me Big Poppa.*" This time Emmy sang out, "*Big Nana, Big Nana, Big Nana.*" We all laughed, and laughed, and laughed. She was so proud of herself. Nana and Papa are what she called my mom and stepfather. She had the best sense of humor.

*****

Emmy was around three years old and Jesse was eighteen months. We were all upstairs and Emmy was not listening. She was pushing my buttons. She often did. I had enough. I put her in time out in a chair in JP's room and told her she was not to move. I walked out of JP's room. I heard the door close behind me. I whipped around and marched back in the room. I scolded Emmy for getting out of the chair after I had told her not to move. She kept telling me she didn't move. I was loudly lecturing her on why she shouldn't lie and why she needed to listen to me. She started to cry. While I was in the middle of scolding her, I saw a movement out of the corner of my eye. Jesse was behind the door. I realized that Emmy had told the truth. She did not move from time out. It was Jesse hiding behind the door. He had pushed the door closed. I felt horrible. I scooped her up. I kept telling her how sorry I was that I had yelled at her and that I didn't believe her. I felt like the worst mother ever. She quickly forgave me and went about playing as if nothing had ever happened. I, on the other hand, was guilt ridden. I think we should all learn something about forgiveness from our children.

*****

Every day on the way home from daycare we would play a game in the car. Emmy would pick the route she wanted us to take home. She usually asked me to go the back roads so we could go over the train tracks. She hoped we would see a train. We passed a huge barn along the way that housed an airplane. We called it the airplane house. She would watch intently for it. If she became distracted and we passed the airplane house without her seeing it, we would need to go back.

My uncle Dave was visiting from Colorado. Emmy went with us to take Uncle Dave back to the Erie airport when it was time for him to return home. We got there early and waited in the car so the kids could see the planes take off and land. Emmy watched for a little while then she said, "Mommy, this is a really, really big airplane house."

*****

Emmy absolutely loved Santa Claus. I have never seen a child love Santa more than she has. Every picture we have of her sitting on his lap shows her with a huge smile, even for her first Christmas when she was only eight months old. She was always hugging or kissing him. Every year we would go to the Christmas tree lighting in town and Santa would ride in on the fire truck. She shook with anticipation and excitement waiting for him. When the fire sirens started, we all sang Christmas carols around the Christmas tree in Marcy Park. Everyone quietly listened. As soon as Emmy realized that Santa was coming, she started jumping up and down and screaming, "Santa, Santa, Santa." She was quite entertaining. People watched her and giggled instead of watching Santa. By September, we started using the classic line, "You better behave, Santa is watching." Once in the grocery store Emmy was being such a stinker. A perfect stranger came up to us and said the same thing. It usually worked to get her to listen and behave.

Once I had told Emmy that she could not have something from the refrigerator. She was angry with me. She said, "Me mad. Me calling Santa on you. You bad, no presents." She went and got the telephone. In her mind she had a conversation with Santa. From that point on whenever Emmy was mad at me, she would say that she was calling Santa.

*****

Emily's Facebook page: https://www.facebook.com/EmmyMott

Emily's Youtube video list:

http://www.youtube.com/watch?v=91dqwuyLLMI

http://www.youtube.com/watch?v=V1X8CtXOSi0

http://www.youtube.com/watch?v=sOk6HUvYcGg

http://www.youtube.com/watch?v=hYEYe2q9Sfc

http://www.youtube.com/watch?v=vujv5H2IlzE

Testimonies

The following testimonies are from Facebook Friends, used with their permission. Thank you. All rights reserved.

Jeannette S. Peterson

Emmy, as the days go by, I keep checking in on you. You have made me cry, knowing what you are going through. I pray for you every day and I know God is with you. He is your protector, you have such a wonderful family, and a very strong one too. I wish I could take all your pain away so that as the days go by you could be pain free. If it was possible I would. ... lifting you in prayer as the angels stand at your side watching over you.

Jennifer King

You know I have always believed in God but not gone to church a whole lot in my life but I have prayed more to God since I found out about Emmy than all the days of my life. I totally fell in love with her the moment I saw her little face and heard her story. She really has had an impact on me. I love her and can't imagine how you all are getting through all of this. I have a hard time understanding why?

Lillian Sanden Glass

My prayers are with the whole family. I have fallen in love with this little girl in only a few months. And since I have never met her, I cannot begin to imagine the depth of your feelings. Emmy is a very special child to have pulled all of us together like this. The love of the Lord shines in her face, her grace and her spirit. I know that because of her and Tammy I now feel closer to God than I have in a long time. I now talk to Him every day and I appreciate things in life I took for granted before. Thank you so much Emmy for letting me into a glimpse of your life and your family. Rest easy precious Emmy, I pray you have no pain. God Bless this precious Angel and all who love her.

Brenda

I know this must be so hard for everyone who has come to love Emmy. Me, included. The family has done so much to hold onto happy memories. I am so thankful that comfort comes from our faith. Emmy is a blessing to everyone because just knowing her smile makes life more precious. That smile will forever be in my heart until one day I can give her a hug in Heaven. Praying for all of you.

Lovingly,

Brenda

Mara

When I read the e-mail, the image came to mind of a butterfly emerging from its chrysalis. When the caterpillar is ready to enter the pupa stage, prior to emerging into the glory of the butterfly, it becomes immobile and is covered in the chrysalis. It seems dormant, seemingly dead in this stage of transformation. When the time comes for the beautiful butterfly to emerge, there is great struggle within the chrysalis. If the chrysalis around the creature would fall away quickly, the butterfly would not emerge into its ultimate form, for in the period of struggle, the butterfly's tender new wings are strengthened: the struggle prepares the wings so they are strong enough to allow flight. At that moment when the wings are ready to fly, the beautiful new creature, in its final form emerges, to the glory of God. It is God who created the caterpillar and it is God who has created the process of transformation from caterpillar to butterfly. Just as one may watch the great struggle the emerging butterfly goes through, we watch with love and compassion the emergence of one we love from this earth's life into a new and eternal life in Jesus. The time now, it seems, is for Emmy who has "Fought the good fight of faith" to begin the final struggle in strengthening her spiritual "wings" as God prepares her to fly in a new world, where she will be stronger and more beautiful and more joyful than she could ever imagine. Jesus is with her in this struggle of His emerging beautiful "butterfly." I pray those who love her and have cared for her in her struggle will take hope and courage in the reality of her transformation and know that someday they will join together with her, face-to-face, in ultimate victory and in newness of eternal life.

In Christ,
Mara

October 2nd, 2012
Tammy Mott

Top Five things I have learned this week from Emmy:

5. There is no such thing as too much Team Umizoomi, Dora, Max and Ruby, Peppa Pig or Bubble Guppies - "Daddy, can you check what is coming on next?"

4. It is okay to jump and roll in a mud puddle wearing brand new white shorts - "Mommy, they will wash."

3. It is okay to turn on the hose and spray your little brother - "He likes it, Mommy."

2. It is okay to eat ice cream every day - "I love ice cream. It is yummy!"

1. It is okay to eat dessert before the meal - "But it is the best part."

*****

November 21, 2012

Diania Kjar Janoski

Good morning Baby Girl and Mott Family. I wish you all a Happy Thanksgiving! Emmy Girl, I send you bundles of kisses and loads of hugs. I pray you can enjoy this turkey day and maybe smile a little while getting a tummy full. :) I will trust in the Father that you have no pain, easy swallowing, and can enjoy your family. I hope you can know how many people, including myself, are thankful for being a part of your life and your family's. You are a very special little girl and God has a special calling on and in your life. I have so much to be thankful for and knowing YOU and your family, even if only thru friends and Facebook, it gives me so much more. I love you Baby Girl. Happy Thanksgiving. :)

Julie K. Haemer-Scott

Whatever challenges I face in a day, Tammy, you are a constant reminder of how irrelevant they are! I know people say everyone has their challenges but your family has touched my life and I will always think of you and your strength and somehow, when faced with any challenge, you have given me reason to see only blessings and small challenges are nothing in comparison! I list you and your beautiful family as blessings in my life! Know how much you are thought of and prayed for throughout the day! Thank you for inspiring me and for making my life's blessings even clearer! So grateful too for the miracle God continues to bless you with each day you hold your daughter!

Kathi Swann

I had never in my life ever been touched by God thru a small child the way I have been touched from Angel Emmy. Thank you Emmy for allowing me to be a part of your life.

Pontine Glioma brain stem cancer kills children. Research has not found a cure. Proceeds from this book will be donated to St. Jude's Children's Research Hospital.

You may also donate to:

http://www.stjude.org

You may send your check to 501 St. Jude Place, Memphis, TN 38105. Please make the check payable to St. Jude Children's Research Hospital.

If you would like to make a gift in honor/memory of someone and would like for St. Jude to send a card acknowledging that a gift has been made to your recipient, you will be asked for the name of the honoree, and the name and address of the card recipient.

To make a secure donation online using your credit or debit card, **visit the St. Jude Gift Shop**.

To donate by phone using a credit or debit card, please call 1-800-873-6983

To donate by mail using a check, credit or debit card, please use our **printable order form** and mail to:

St. Jude Holiday Card Program
P.O. Box 1000, Dept. 142
Memphis, TN 38148-0142

When late entertainer Danny Thomas opened the doors to St. Jude Children's Research Hospital in 1962, he was not just changing the lives of children who would walk through its doors—he was changing lives across the world. When St. Jude completed its $1 billion, five-year expansion in 2005, it bolstered the hospital's efforts to find cures for the catastrophic diseases of childhood. Now with the addition of the Chili's Care Center, a larger, rejuvenated Kay Kafe cafeteria for employees and patients, and renovations to the medicine room and rehabilitation areas, the hospital is more poised than ever to advance cures, and means of prevention, for pediatric catastrophic diseases through research and treatment.

Ride4thEM: http://ride4them.org/

What started as a way to raise money for one local family, has turned into an annual event to raise money for families in Northeastern Ohio and Northwestern Pennsylvania stricken by the financial burdens of caring for a child with a life threatening illness. The event takes place on the last Saturday of July every year and is held at Pymatuning State Park Main Beach in Andover, OH. There's a little something for everyone, including a Century (100 mile) Bike Ride, a 25 mile Bike Ride, a 5k Run/Walk, a Coed 4's Sand Volleyball Tournament, a Motorcycle Run, a Kid's Bicycle Ride/Safety Zone, a Chinese Auction, a 50/50 Raffle, Kid's Activities Tent, Great Food, Great Entertainment, and much, much more!!

Bike Ride (Christy Paul): cycling@ride4them.org

5k (Kelly Summers): 5k@ride4them.org

Volleyball Tournament (Diana Snodgrass): volleyball@ride4them.org

Motorcycle Run (Adam Cook): motorcycle@ride4them.org

Kid's Bike Ride/Safety Zone (Cody Paul): kidscycling@ride4them.org

Chinese Auction (Christine Claypoole): chineseauction@ride4them.org

General Questions: info@ride4them.org

Build-A-Bear Workshop®

At Build-A-Bear Workshop®, our mission is to bring the Teddy Bear to life. An American icon, the Teddy Bear brings to mind warm thoughts about our childhood, about friendship, about trust and comfort, and also about love. Build-A-Bear Workshop embodies those thoughts in how we run our business everyday. Stores located across the US and in many international sites, as well as online.

Make-A-Wish Foundation®

http://www.wish.org/

Since 1980, the Make-A-Wish Foundation® has enriched the lives of children with life-threatening medical conditions through its wish-granting work. The Foundation's mission reflects the life-changing impact that a Make-A-Wish® experience has on children, families, referral sources, donors, sponsors and entire communities.

The Make-A-Wish Foundation was founded in 1980 after a little boy named Chris Greicius realized his heartfelt wish to become a police officer. Since its humble beginnings, the organization has blossomed into a worldwide phenomenon, reaching more than 250,000 children around the world.

Although it has become one of the world's most well-known charities, the Make-A-Wish Foundation has maintained the grassroots fulfillment of its mission.

A network of nearly 25,000 volunteers enable the Make-A-Wish Foundation to serve children with life-threatening medical conditions. Volunteers serve as wish granters, fundraisers, special events assistants and in numerous other capacities.

As the Foundation continues to mature, its mission will remain steadfast. Wish children of the past, present and future will have an opportunity to **share the power of a wish®**.

Catholic Charities: http://www.catholiccharitiesdc.org/PAS
Pregnancy and Adoptions

924 G St., NW, Washington DC (Downtown)
(202) 772-4300 FREE (202) 772-4300 ext. 041 | fax (202) 526-1829

4601 Presidents Dr., Suite 215, Lanham, MD 20706
(301) 731-4703 FREE (301) 731-4703 ext. 308 | fax (301) 731-6634

12247 Georgia Ave., Silver Spring, MD
(301) 942-1790 FREE (301) 942-1790 | fax (301) 949-1371

More books
By
Carolinas Ecumenical Healing Ministries
On
Amazon.com

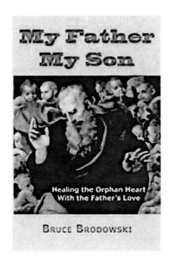

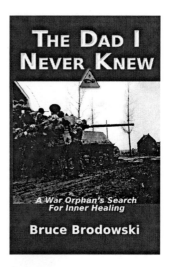

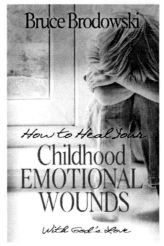

2013

CPSIA information can be obtained at www.ICGtesting.com
Printed in the USA
BVOW070923260213

314219BV00001BA/4/P

9 780982 658130